CAMBRIDGE LIBRARY COLLECTION

Books of enduring scholarly value

History of Printing, Publishing and Libraries

The interface between authors and their readers is a fascinating subject in its own right, revealing a great deal about social attitudes, technological progress, aesthetic values, fashionable interests, political positions, economic constraints, and individual personalities. This part of the Cambridge Library Collection reissues classic studies in the area of printing and publishing history that shed light on developments in typography and book design, printing and binding, the rise and fall of publishing houses and periodicals, and the roles of authors and illustrators. It documents the ebb and flow of the book trade supplying a wide range of customers with products from almanacs to novels, bibles to erotica, and poetry to statistics.

The Enemies of Books

First published in 1881, this popular and entertaining work by the printer and bibliographer William Blades (1824–90) examines the numerous threats that books have faced throughout their existence. Based on the author's experience of collecting printed works, the book explores such destructive forces as fire, water, disgruntled pirates, ignorance, and vermin. Even bookbinders and collectors are accused of causing mischief. In 1886, Blades was cruelly tormented by one of his enemies when his printing works burned down. A founder of the Library Association, he most notably investigated the work of Caxton: his two-volume *Life and Typography of William Caxton* (1861–3) is also reissued in this series. After his death, his extensive collection of books formed the basis of the St Bride Printing Library. Six editions of *The Enemies of Books* emerged between 1881 and 1886. Reissued here is the revised, enlarged and illustrated version that appeared in 1888.

Cambridge University Press has long been a pioneer in the reissuing of out-of-print titles from its own backlist, producing digital reprints of books that are still sought after by scholars and students but could not be reprinted economically using traditional technology. The Cambridge Library Collection extends this activity to a wider range of books which are still of importance to researchers and professionals, either for the source material they contain, or as landmarks in the history of their academic discipline.

Drawing from the world-renowned collections in the Cambridge University Library and other partner libraries, and guided by the advice of experts in each subject area, Cambridge University Press is using state-of-the-art scanning machines in its own Printing House to capture the content of each book selected for inclusion. The files are processed to give a consistently clear, crisp image, and the books finished to the high quality standard for which the Press is recognised around the world. The latest print-on-demand technology ensures that the books will remain available indefinitely, and that orders for single or multiple copies can quickly be supplied.

The Cambridge Library Collection brings back to life books of enduring scholarly value (including out-of-copyright works originally issued by other publishers) across a wide range of disciplines in the humanities and social sciences and in science and technology.

The Enemies of Books

William Blades

University Printing House, Cambridge, CB2 8BS, United Kingdom

Cambridge University Press is part of the University of Cambridge.
It furthers the University's mission by disseminating knowledge in the pursuit of education, learning and research at the highest international levels of excellence.

www.cambridge.org
Information on this title: www.cambridge.org/9781108076418

This edition first published 1888
This digitally printed version 2015

ISBN 978-1-108-07641-8 Paperback

RISE · PRAY · WORK

The Book-Lover's Library.

Edited by

Henry B. Wheatley, F.S.A.

Servant using a "Caxton" to light the Fire.

THE

ENEMIES OF BOOKS

BY

WILLIAM BLADES

Revised and Enlarged by the Author

LONDON

ELLIOT STOCK, 62 PATERNOSTER ROW

1888

CONTENTS.

CHAPTER I.

Fire.

CHAPTER II.

WATER.

CHAPTER III.

GAS AND HEAT.

CHAPTER IV.

Dust and Neglect.

CHAPTER V.

Ignorance and Bigotry.

CHAPTER VI.

The Bookworm.

CHAPTER VII.

Other Vermin.

CHAPTER VIII.

Bookbinders.

CHAPTER IX.

COLLECTORS.

CHAPTER X.

Servants and Children.

Postscriptum.

Conclusion.

ILLUSTRATIONS.

THE ENEMIES OF BOOKS.

CHAPTER I.

FIRE.

HERE are many of the forces of Nature which tend to injure Books; but among them all not one has been half so destructive as Fire. It would be tedious to write out a bare list only of the numerous libraries and bibliographical treasures which, in one way or another, have been seized by the Fire-king as his own. Chance conflagrations, fanatic incendiarism, Judicial bonfires, and even

household stoves have, time after time, thinned the treasures as well as the rubbish of past ages, until, probably, not one thousandth part of the books that have been are still extant. This destruction cannot, however, be reckoned as all loss; for had not the "cleansing fires" removed mountains of rubbish from our midst, strong destructive measures would have become a necessity from sheer want of space in which to store so many volumes.

Before the invention of Printing, books were comparatively scarce; and, knowing as we do, how very difficult it is, even after the steam-press has been working for half a century, to make a collection of half a million books, we are forced to receive with great incredulity the accounts in old writers of the wonderful extent of ancient libraries.

The historian Gibbon, very incredulous in many things, accepts without questioning the fables told upon this subject. No doubt the libraries of MSS. collected generation after generation by the Egyptian Ptolemies became, in the course of time, the most extensive ever then known; and were famous throughout the world for the costliness of their ornamentation, and importance of their untold contents. Two of these were at Alexandria, the larger of which was in the quarter called Bruchium. These volumes, like all manuscripts of those early ages, were written on sheets of parchment, having a wooden roller at each end so that the reader needed only to unroll a portion at a time. During Cæsar's Alexandrian War, B.C. 48, the larger collection was consumed by fire and again burnt by the Saracens in A.D. 640. An immense loss was inflicted upon mankind thereby; but when we are told of 700,000, or even 500,000 of such volumes being destroyed we instinctively feel that such numbers must be a great exaggeration. Equally incredulous must we be when we read of half a million volumes being burnt at Carthage some centuries later, and other similar accounts.

Among the earliest records of the wholesale destruction of Books is that narrated by St. Luke, when, after the preaching of Paul, many of the Ephesians "which used curious arts brought their books together, and burned them before all men: and they counted the price of them, and found it 50,000 pieces of silver" (Acts xix, 19). Doubtless these books of idolatrous divination and alchemy, of enchantments and witchcraft, were righteously destroyed by those to whom they had been and might again be spiritually injurious; and doubtless had they escaped the fire then, not one of them would have survived to the present time, no MS. of that age being now extant. Nevertheless, I must confess to a certain amount of mental disquietude and uneasiness when I think of books worth 50,000 denarii—or, speaking roughly, say £18,750,[1] of our modern money being made into bonfires. What curious illustrations of early heathenism, of Devil worship, of Serpent worship, of Sun worship, and other archaic forms of religion; of early astrological and chemical lore, derived from the Egyptians, the Persians, the Greeks; what abundance of superstitious observances and what is now termed "Folk-lore"; what riches, too, for the philological student, did those many books contain, and how famous would the library now be that could boast of possessing but a few of them.

[1] The received opinion is that the "pieces of silver" here mentioned were Roman denarii, which were the silver pieces then commonly used in Ephesus. If now we weigh a denarius against modern silver, it is exactly equal to ninepence, and fifty thousand times ninepence gives £1,875. It is always a difficult matter to arrive at a just estimate of the relative value of the same coin in different ages; but reckoning that money then had at least ten times the purchasing value of money now, we arrive at what was probably about the value of the magical books burnt, viz.: £18,750.

The ruins of Ephesus bear unimpeachable evidence that the City was very extensive and had magnificent buildings. It was one of the free cities, governing itself. Its trade in shrines and idols was very extensive, being spread through all known lands. There the magical arts were remarkably prevalent, and notwithstanding the numerous converts made by the early Christians, the 'Εφέσια γράμματα, or little scrolls upon which magic sentences were written, formed an extensive trade up to the fourth century. These "writings" were used for divination, as a protection against the "evil eye," and generally as charms against all evil. They were carried about the person, so that probably thousands of them were thrown into the flames by St. Paul's hearers when his glowing words convinced them of their superstition.

Imagine an open space near the grand Temple of Diana, with fine buildings around. Slightly raised above the crowd, the Apostle, preaching with great power and persuasion concerning superstition, holds in thrall the assembled multitude. On the outskirts of the crowd are numerous bonfires, upon which Jew and Gentile are throwing into the flames bundle upon bundle of scrolls, while an Asiarch with his peace-officers looks on with the conventional stolidity of policemen in all ages and all nations. It must have been an impressive scene, and many a worse subject has been chosen for the walls of the Royal Academy.

Books in those early times, whether orthodox or heterodox, appear to have had a precarious existence. The heathens at each fresh outbreak of persecution burnt all the Christian writings they could find, and the Christians, when they got the upper hand, retaliated with interest upon the pagan literature. The Mohammedan reason for destroying books—"If they contain what is in the Koran they are superfluous, and if they contain anything opposed to it they are immoral," seems, indeed, *mutatis mutandis*, to have been the general rule for all such devastators.

The Invention of Printing made the entire destruction of any author's works much more difficult, so quickly and so extensively did books spread through all lands. On the other hand, as books multiplied, so did destruction go hand in hand with production, and soon were printed books doomed to suffer in the same penal fires, that up to then had been fed on MSS. only.

At Cremona, in 1569, 12,000 books printed in Hebrew were publicly burnt as heretical, simply on account of their language; and Cardinal Ximenes, at the capture of Granada, treated 5,000 copies of the Koran in the same way.

At the time of the Reformation in England a great destruction of books took place.

The antiquarian Bale, writing in 1587, thus speaks of the shameful fate of the Monastic libraries :—

"A greate nombre of them whyche purchased those superstycyouse mansyons (*Monasteries*) reserved of those librarye bookes some to serve their jakes, some to scoure theyr candelstyckes, and some to rubbe theyr bootes. Some they solde to the grossers and sope sellers, and some they sent over see to ye booke bynders, not in small nombre, but at tymes whole shyppes full, to ye wonderynge of foren nacyons. Yea ye Universytees of thys realme are not alle clere in thys detestable fact. But cursed is that bellye whyche seketh to be fedde with suche ungodlye gaynes, and so depelye shameth hys natural conterye. I knowe a merchant manne, whych shall at thys tyme be namelesse, that boughte ye contentes of two noble lybraryes for forty shyllynges pryce : a shame it is to be spoken. Thys stuffe hathe he occupyed in ye stede of greye paper, by ye space of more than these ten yeares, and yet he hathe store ynoughe for as manye years to come. A prodygyous example is thys, and to be abhorred of all men whyche love theyr nacyon as they shoulde do. The monkes kepte them undre dust, ye ydle-headed prestes regarded them not, theyr latter owners have most shamefully abused them, and ye covetouse merchantes have solde them away into foren nacyons for moneye."

How the imagination recoils at the idea of Caxton's translation of the Metamorphoses of Ovid, or perhaps his "Lyf of therle of Oxenforde," together with many another book from our first presses, not a fragment of which do we now possess, being used for baking "pyes."

At the Great Fire of London in 1666, the number of books burnt was enormous. Not only in private houses and Corporate and Church libraries were priceless collections reduced to cinders, but an immense stock of books removed from Paternoster Row by the Stationers for safety was burnt to ashes in the vaults of St. Paul's Cathedral.

Coming nearer to our own day, how thankful we ought to be for the preservation of the Cotton Library. Great was the consternation in the literary world of 1731 when they heard of the fire at Ashburnham House, Westminster, where, at that time, the Cotton MSS. were deposited. By great exertions the fire was conquered, but not before many MSS. had been quite destroyed and many others injured. Much skill was shown in the partial restoration of these books, charred almost beyond recognition; they were carefully separated leaf by leaf, soaked in a chemical solution, and then pressed flat between sheets of transparent paper. A curious heap of scorched leaves, previous to any treatment, and looking like a monster wasps' nest, may be seen in a glass case in the MS. department of the British Museum, showing the condition to which many other volumes had been reduced.

Just a hundred years ago the mob, in the "Birmingham Riots," burnt the valuable library of Dr. Priestley, and in the "Gordon Riots" were burnt the literary and other collections of Lord Mansfield, the celebrated judge, he who had the courage first to decide that the Slave who reached the English shore was thenceforward a free man. The loss of the latter library drew from the poet Cowper two short and weak poems. The poet first deplores the destruction of the valuable printed books, and then the irretrievable loss to history by the burning of his Lordship's many personal manuscripts and contemporary documents.

> "Their pages mangled, burnt and torn,
> The loss was his alone;
> But ages yet to come shall mourn
> The burning of his own."

The second poem commences with the following doggerel:—

> "When Wit and Genius meet their doom
> In all-devouring Flame,
> They tell us of the Fate of Rome
> And bid us fear the same."

The much finer and more extensive library of Dr. Priestley was left unnoticed and unlamented by the orthodox poet, who probably felt a complacent satisfaction at the destruction of heterodox books, the owner being an Unitarian Minister.

The magnificent library of Strasbourg was burnt by the shells of the German Army in 1870. Then disappeared for ever, together with other unique documents, the original records of the famous law-suits between Gutenberg, one of the first Printers, and his partners, upon the right understanding of which depends the claim of Gutenberg to the invention of the Art. The flames raged between high brick walls, roaring louder than a blast furnace. Seldom, indeed, have Mars and Pluto had so dainty a sacrifice offered at their shrines; for over all the din of battle, and the reverberation of monster artillery, the burning leaves of the first printed Bible and many another priceless volume were wafted into the sky, the ashes floating for miles on the heated air, and carrying to the astonished countryman the first news of the devastation of his Capital.

When the Offor Collection was put to the hammer by Messrs Sotheby and Wilkinson, the well-known auctioneers of Wellington Street, and when about three days of the sale had been gone through, a Fire occurred in the adjoining house, and, gaining possession of the Sale Rooms, made a speedy end of the unique Bunyan and other rarities then on show. I was allowed to see the Ruins on the following day, and by means of a ladder and some scrambling managed to enter the Sale Room where parts of the floor still remained. It was a fearful sight those scorched rows of Volumes still on the shelves; and curious was it to notice how the flames, burning off the backs of the books first, had then run up behind the shelves, and so attacked the fore-edge of the volumes standing upon them, leaving the majority with a perfectly untouched oval centre of white paper and plain print, while the whole surrounding parts were but a mass of black cinders. The salvage was sold in one lot for a small sum, and the purchaser, after a good deal of sorting and mending and binding placed about 1,000 volumes for sale at Messrs. Puttick and Simpson's in the following year.

So, too, when the curious old Library which was in a gallery of the Dutch Church, Austin Friars, was nearly destroyed in the fire which devastated the Church in 1862, the books which escaped were sadly injured. Not long before I had spent some hours there hunting for English Fifteenth-century Books, and shall never forget the state of dirt in which I came away. Without anyone to care for them, the books had remained untouched for many a decade—damp dust, half an inch thick, having settled upon them! Then came the fire, and while the roof was all ablaze streams of hot water, like a boiling deluge washed down upon them. The wonder was they were not turned into a muddy pulp. After all was over, the whole of the library, no portion of which could legally be given away, was *lent for ever* to the Corporation of London. Scorched and sodden, the salvage came into the hands of Mr. Overall, their indefatigable librarian. In a hired attic, he hung up the volumes that would bear it over strings like clothes, to dry, and there for weeks and weeks were the stained, distorted volumes, often without covers, often in single leaves, carefully tended and dry-nursed. Washing, sizing, pressing, and binding effected wonders, and no one who to-day looks upon the attractive little alcove in the Guildhall Library labelled "Bibliotheca Ecclesiæ Londino-Belgicæ" and sees the rows of handsomely-lettered backs, could imagine that not long ago this, the most curious portion of the City's literary collections, was in a state when a five-pound note would have seemed more than full value for the lot.

CHAPTER II.

WATER.

EXT to Fire we must rank Water in its two forms, liquid and vapour, as the greatest destroyer of books. Thousands of volumes have been actually drowned at Sea, and no more heard of them than of the Sailors to whose charge they were committed. D'Israeli narrates that, about the year 1700, Heer Hudde, an opulent burgomaster of Middleburgh, travelled for 30 years disguised as a mandarin, throughout the length and breadth of the Celestial Empire. Everywhere he collected books, and his extensive literary treasures were at length safely shipped for transmission to Europe, but, to the irreparable loss of his native country, they never reached their destination, the vessel having foundered in a storm.

In 1785 died the famous Maffei Pinelli, whose library was celebrated throughout the world. It had been collected by the Pinelli family for many generations and comprised an extraordinary number of Greek, Latin, and Italian works, many of them first editions, beautifully illuminated, together with numerous MSS. dating from the 11th to the 16th century. The whole library was sold by the Executors to Mr. Edwards, bookseller, of Pall Mall, who placed the volumes in three vessels for transport from Venice to London. Pursued by Corsairs, one of the vessels was captured, but the pirate, disgusted at not finding any treasure, threw all the books into the sea. The other two vessels escaped and

Water.

delivered their freight safely, and in 1789-90 the books which had been so near destruction were sold at the great room in Conduit Street, for more than £9,000.

These pirates were more excusable than Mohammed II who, upon the capture of Constantinople in the 15th century, after giving up the devoted city to be sacked by his licentious soldiers, ordered the books in all the churches as well as the great library of the Emperor Constantine, containing 120,000 Manuscripts, to be thrown into the sea.

In the shape of rain, water has frequently caused irreparable injury. Positive wet is fortunately of rare occurrence in a library, but is very destructive when it does come, and, if long continued, the substance of the paper succumbs to the unhealthy influence and rots and rots until all fibre disappears, and the paper is reduced to a white decay which crumbles into powder when handled.

Few old libraries in England are now so thoroughly neglected as they were thirty years ago. The state of many of our Collegiate and Cathedral libraries was at that time simply appalling. I could mention many instances, one especially, where a window having been left broken for a long time, the ivy had pushed through and crept over a row of books, each of which was worth hundreds of pounds. In rainy weather the water was conducted, as by a pipe, along the tops of the books and soaked through the whole.

In another and smaller collection, the rain came straight on to a book-case through a sky-light, saturating continually the top shelf containing Caxtons and other early English books, one of which, although rotten, was sold soon after by permission of the Charity Commissioners for £200.

Germany, too, the very birth-place of Printing, allows similar destruction to go on unchecked, if the following letter, which appeared about a year ago (1879) in the *Academy* has any truth in it :—

"For some time past the condition of the library at Wolfenbuttel has been most disgraceful. The building is in so unsafe a condition that portions of the walls and ceilings have fallen in, and the many treasures in Books and MSS. contained in it are exposed to damp and decay. An appeal has been issued that this valuable collection may not be allowed to perish for want of funds, and that it may also be now at length removed to Brunswick, since Wolfenbuttel is entirely deserted as an intellectual centre. No false sentimentality regarding the memory of its former custodians, Leibnitz and Lessing, should hinder this project. Lessing himself would have been the first to urge that the library and its utility should be considered above all things."

The collection of books at Wolfenbuttel is simply magnificent, and I cannot but hope the above report was exaggerated. Were these books to be injured for the want of a small sum spent on the roof, it would be a lasting disgrace to the nation. There are so many genuine book-lovers in Fatherland that the commission of such a crime would seem incredible, did not bibliographical history teem with similar desecrations.[1]

Water in the form of vapour is a great enemy of books, the damp attacking both outside and inside. Outside it fosters the growth of a white mould or fungus which vegetates upon the edges of the leaves, upon the sides and in the joints of the binding. It is easily wiped off, but not without leaving a plain mark, where the mould-spots have been. Under the microscope a mould-spot is seen to be a miniature forest of lovely trees, covered with a beautiful white foliage, upas trees whose roots are embedded in the leather and destroy its texture.

Inside the book, damp encourages the growth of those ugly brown spots which so often disfigure prints and "livres de luxe." Especially it attacks books printed

[1] This was written in 1879, since which time a new building has been erected.

in the early part of this century, when paper-makers had just discovered that they could bleach their rags, and perfectly white paper, well pressed after printing, had become the fashion. This paper from the inefficient means used to neutralise the bleach, carried the seeds of decay in itself, and when exposed to any damp soon became discoloured with brown stains. Dr. Dibdin's extravagant bibliographical works are mostly so injured; and although the Doctor's bibliography is very incorrect, and his spun-out inanities and wearisome affectations often annoy one, yet his books are so beautifully illustrated, and he is so full of personal anecdote and chit chat, that it grieves the heart to see "foxey" stains common in his most superb works.

In a perfectly dry and warm library these spots would probably remain undeveloped, but many endowed as well as private libraries are not in daily use, and are often injured from a false idea that a hard frost and prolonged cold do no injury to a library so long as the weather is dry. The fact is that books should never be allowed to get really cold, for when a thaw comes and the weather sets in warm, the air, laden with damp, penetrates the inmost recesses, and working its way between the volumes and even between the leaves, deposits upon their cold surface its moisture. The best preventative of this is a warm atmosphere during the frost, sudden heating when the frost has gone being useless.

Our worst enemies are sometimes our real friends, and perhaps the best way of keeping libraries entirely free from damp is to circulate our enemy in the shape of hot water through pipes laid under the floor. The facilities now offered for heating such pipes from the outside are so great, the expense comparatively so small, and the direct gain in the expulsion of damp so decided, that where it can be accomplished without much trouble it is well worth the doing.

At the same time no system of heating should be allowed to supersede the open grate, which supplies a ventilation to the room as useful to the health of the books as to the health of the occupier. A coal fire is objectionable on many grounds. It is dangerous, dirty and dusty. On the other hand an asbestos fire, where the lumps are judiciously laid, gives all the warmth and ventilation of a common fire without any of its annoyances; and to any one who loves to be independent of servants, and to know that, however deeply he may sleep over his "copy," his fire will not fail to keep awake, an asbestos stove is invaluable.

It is a mistake also to imagine that keeping the best bound volumes in a glass doored book-case is a preservative. The damp air will certainly penetrate, and as the absence of ventilation will assist the formation of mould, the books will be worse off than if they had been placed in open shelves. If security be desirable, by all means abolish the glass and place ornamental brass wire-work in its stead. Like the writers of old Cookery Books who stamped special receipts with the testimony of personal experience, I can say "probatum est."

CHAPTER III.

Gas and Heat.

HAT a valuable servant is Gas, and how dreadfully we should cry out were it to be banished from our homes; and yet no one who loves his books should allow a single jet in his library, unless, indeed he can afford a "sun light," which is the form in which it is used in some public libraries, where the whole of the fumes are carried at once into the open air.

Unfortunately, I can speak from experience of the dire effect of gas in a confined space. Some years ago when placing the shelves round the small room, which, by a euphemism, is called my library, I took the precaution of making two self-acting ventilators which communicated directly with the outer air just under the ceiling. For economy of space as well as of temper (for lamps of all kinds are sore trials), I had a gasalier of three lights over the table. The effect was to cause great heat in the upper regions, and in the course of a year or two the leather valence which hung from the window, as well as the fringe which dropped half-an-inch from each shelf to keep out the dust, was just like tinder, and in some parts actually fell to the ground by its own weight; while the backs of the books upon the top shelves were perished, and crumbled away when touched, being reduced to the consistency of Scotch snuff. This was, of course, due to the sulphur in the gas fumes, which attack russia quickest, while calf and morocco suffer not quite so much. I remember having a book some years ago from the top shelf in the library of the London

Institution, where gas is used, and the whole of the back fell off in my hands, although the volume in other respects seemed quite uninjured. Thousands more were in a similar plight.

As the paper of the volumes is uninjured, it might be objected that, after all, gas is not so much the enemy of the book itself as of its covering; but then, re-binding always leaves a book smaller, and often deprives it of leaves at the beginning or end, which the binder's wisdom has thought useless. Oh! the havoc I have seen committed by binders. You may assume your most impressive aspect—you may write down your instructions as if you were making your last will and testament—you may swear you will not pay if your books are ploughed—'tis all in vain—the creed of a binder is very short, and comprised in a single article, and that article is the one vile word "Shavings." But not now will I follow this depressing subject; binders, as enemies of books, deserve, and shall have, a whole chapter to themselves.

It is much easier to decry gas than to find a remedy. Sun lights require especial arrangements, and are very expensive on account of the quantity of gas consumed. The library illumination of the future promises to be the electric light. If only steady and moderate in price, it would be a great boon to public libraries, and perhaps the day is not far distant when it will replace gas, even in private houses. That will, indeed, be a day of jubilee to the literary labourer. The injury done by gas is so generally acknowledged by the heads of our national libraries, that it is strictly excluded from their domains, although the danger from explosion and fire, even if the results of combustion were innocuous, would be sufficient cause for its banishment.

The electric light has been in use for some months in the Reading Room of the British

Museum, and is a great boon to the readers. The light is not quite equally diffused, and you must choose particular positions if you want to work happily. There is a great objection, too, in the humming fizz which accompanies the action of the electricity. There is a still greater objection when small pieces of hot chalk fall on your bald head, an annoyance which has been lately (1880) entirely removed by placing a receptacle beneath each burner. You require also to become accustomed to the whiteness of the light before you can altogether forget it. But with all its faults it confers a great boon upon students, enabling them not only to work three hours longer in the winter-time, but restoring to them the use of foggy and dark days, in which formerly no book-work at all could be pursued.[1]

[1] 1887. The system in use is still "Siemens," but, owing to long experience and improvements, is not now open to the above objections.

Heat alone, without any noxious fumes, is, if continuous, very injurious to books, and, without gas, bindings may be utterly destroyed by desiccation, the leather losing all its natural oils by long exposure to much heat. It is, therefore, a great pity to place books high up in a room where heat of any kind is used, for it must rise to the top, and if sufficient to be of comfort to the readers below, is certain to be hot enough above to injure the bindings.

The surest way to preserve your books in health is to treat them as you would your own children, who are sure to sicken if confined in an atmosphere which is impure, too hot, too cold, too damp, or too dry. It is just the same with the progeny of literature.

If any credence may be given to Monkish legends, books have sometimes been preserved in this world, only to meet a desiccating fate in the world to come. The story is probably an invention of the enemy to throw discredit on the learning and ability of the preaching

Friars with Books.

Friars, an Order which was at constant war with the illiterate secular Clergy. It runs thus:—"In the year 1439, two Minorite friars who had all their lives collected books, died. In accordance with popular belief, they were at once conducted before the heavenly tribunal to hear their doom, taking with them two asses laden with books. At Heaven's gate the porter demanded, 'Whence came ye?' The Minorites replied 'From a monastery of St. Francis.' 'Oh!' said the porter, 'then St. Francis shall be your judge.' So that saint was summoned, and at sight of the friars and their burden demanded who they were, and why they had brought so many books with them. 'We are Minorites,' they humbly replied, 'and we have brought these few books with us as a solatium in the new Jerusalem.' 'And you, when on earth, practised the good they teach?' sternly demanded the saint, who read their characters at a glance. Their faltering reply was sufficient, and the blessed saint at once passed judgment as follows:—'Insomuch as, seduced by a foolish vanity, and against your vows of poverty, you have amassed this multitude of books and thereby and therefor have neglected the duties and broken the rules of your Order, you are now sentenced to read your books for ever and ever in the fires of Hell.' Immediately, a roaring noise filled the air, and a flaming chasm opened in which friars, and asses and books were suddenly engulphed."

CHAPTER IV.

Dust and Neglect.

UST upon Books to any extent points to neglect, and neglect means more or less slow Decay.

A well-gilt top to a book is a great preventive against damage by dust, while to leave books with rough tops and unprotected is sure to produce stains and dirty margins.

In olden times, when few persons had private collections of books, the collegiate and corporate libraries were of great use to students. The librarians' duties were then no sinecure, and there was little opportunity for dust to find a resting-place. The

Nineteenth Century and the Steam Press ushered in a new era. By degrees the libraries which were unendowed fell behind the age, and were consequently neglected. No new works found their way in, and the obsolete old books were left uncared for and unvisited. I have seen many old libraries, the doors of which remained unopened from week's end to week's end; where you inhaled the dust of paper-decay with every breath, and could not take up a book without sneezing; where old boxes, full of older literature, served as preserves for the bookworm, without even an autumn "battue" to thin the breed. Occasionally these libraries were (I speak of thirty years ago) put even to vile uses, such as would have shocked all ideas of propriety could our ancestors have foreseen their fate.

I recall vividly a bright summer morning many years ago, when, in search of Caxtons, I entered the inner quadrangle of a certain wealthy College in one of our learned Universities. The buildings around were charming in their grey tones and shady nooks. They had a noble history, too, and their scholarly sons were (and are) not unworthy successors of their ancestral renown. The sun shone warmly, and most of the casements were open. From one came curling a whiff of tobacco; from another the hum of conversation; from a third the tones of a piano. A couple of undergraduates sauntered on the shady side, arm in arm, with broken caps and torn gowns — proud insignia of their last term. The grey stone walls were covered with ivy, except where an old dial with its antiquated Latin inscription kept count of the sun's ascent. The chapel on one side, only distinguishable from the "rooms" by the shape of its windows, seemed to keep watch over the morality of the foundation, just as the dining-hall opposite, from whence issued a white-aproned cook, did of its worldly prosperity. As you trod the level pavement, you passed comfortable—nay, dainty—apartments, where lace curtains at the windows, antimacassars on the chairs, the silver biscuit-box and the thin-stemmed wine-glass moderated academic toils. Gilt-backed books on gilded shelf or table caught the eye, and as you turned your glance from the luxurious interiors to the well-shorn lawn in the Quad., with its classic fountain also gilded by sunbeams, the mental vision saw plainly written over the whole "The Union of Luxury and Learning."

Surely here, thought I, if anywhere, the old world literature will be valued and nursed with gracious care; so with a pleasing sense of the general congruity of all around me, I enquired for the rooms of the librarian. Nobody seemed to be quite sure of his name, or upon whom the bibliographical mantle had descended. His post, it seemed, was honorary and a sinecure, being imposed, as a rule, upon the youngest "Fellow." No one cared for the appointment, and as a matter of course the keys of office had but distant acquaintance with the lock. At last I was rewarded with success, and politely, but mutely, conducted by the librarian into his kingdom of dust and silence. The dark portraits of past benefactors looked after us from their dusty old frames in dim astonishment as we passed, evidently wondering whether we meant "work"; book-decay—that peculiar flavour which haunts certain libraries—was heavy in the air, the floor was dusty, making the sunbeams as we passed bright with atoms; the shelves were dusty, the "stands" in the middle were thick with dust, the old leather table in the bow window, and the chairs on either side, were very dusty. Replying to a question, my conductor thought there was a manuscript catalogue of the Library somewhere, but thought, also, that it was not easy to find any books by it, and he knew not at the minute where to put his hand upon it. The Library, he said, was of little use now, as the Fellows had their own books and very seldom required 17th and 18th century editions, and no new books had been added to the collection for a long time.

We passed down a few steps into an inner library where piles of early folios were wasting away on the ground. Beneath an old ebony table were two long carved oak chests. I lifted the lid of one, and at the top was a once-white surplice covered with dust, and beneath was a mass of tracts—Commonwealth quartos, unbound—a prey to worms and decay. All was neglect. The outer door of this room, which was open, was nearly on a level with the Quadrangle; some coats, and trousers, and boots were upon the ebony table, and a "gyp" was brushing away at them just within the door—in wet weather he performed these

Dust.

functions entirely within the library—as innocent of the incongruity of his position as my guide himself. Oh! Richard of Bury, I sighed, for a sharp stone from your sling to pierce with indignant sarcasm the mental armour of these College dullards.

Happily, things are altered now, and the disgrace of such neglect no longer hangs on the College. Let us hope, in these days of revived respect for antiquity, no other College library is in a similar plight.

Not Englishmen alone are guilty, however, of such unloving treatment of their bibliographical treasures. The following is translated from an interesting work just published in Paris,[1] and shows how, even at this very time, and in the centre of the literary activity of France, books meet their fate.

[1] Le luxe des Livres par L. Derome. 8vo, Paris, 1879.

M. Derome loquitur:—

"Let us now enter the communal library of some large provincial town. The interior has a lamentable appearance; dust and disorder have made it their home. It has a librarian, but he has the consideration of a porter only, and goes but once a week to see the state of the books committed to his care; they are in a bad state, piled in heaps and perishing in corners for want of attention and binding. At this present time (1879) more than one public library in Paris could be mentioned in which thousands of books are received annually, all of which will have disappeared in the course of 50 years or so for want of binding; there are rare books, impossible to replace, falling to pieces because no care is given to them, that is to say, they are left unbound, a prey to dust and the worm, and cannot be touched without dismemberment."

All history shows that this neglect belongs not to any particular age or nation. I extract the following story from Edmond Werdet's "Histoire du Livre." [1]

"The Poet Boccaccio, when travelling in Apulia, was anxious to visit the celebrated Convent of Mount

[1] "Histoire du Livre en France," par E. Werdet. 8vo, Paris, 1851.

Cassin, especially to see its library, of which he had heard much. He accosted, with great courtesy, one of the monks whose countenance attracted him, and begged him to have the kindness to show him the library. 'See for yourself,' said the monk, brusquely, pointing at the same time to an old stone staircase, broken with age. Boccaccio hastily mounted in great joy at the prospect of a grand bibliographical treat. Soon he reached the room, which was without key or even door as protection to its treasures. What was his astonishment to see that the grass growing in the window-sills actually darkened the room, and that all the books and seats were an inch thick in dust. In utter astonishment he lifted one book after another. All were manuscripts of extreme antiquity, but all were dreadfully dilapidated. Many had lost whole sections which had been violently extracted, and in many all the blank margins of the vellum had been cut away. In fact, the mutilation was thorough.

"Grieved at seeing the work and the wisdom of so many illustrious men fallen into the hands of custodians so unworthy, Boccaccio descended with tears in his eyes. In the cloisters he met another monk, and enquired of him how the MSS. had become so mutilated. 'Oh!' he replied, 'we are obliged, you know, to earn a few sous for our needs, so we cut away the blank margins of the manuscripts for writing upon, and make of them small books of devotion, which we sell to women and children."

As a postscript to this story, Mr. Timmins, of Birmingham, informs me that the treasures of the Monte Cassino Library are better cared for now than in Boccàccio's days, the worthy prior being proud of his valuable MSS. and very willing to show them. It will interest many readers to know that there is now a complete printing office, lithographic as well as typographic, at full work in one large room of the Monastery, where their wonderful MS. of Dante has been already reprinted, and where other fac-simile works are now in progress.

CHAPTER V.

Ignorance and Bigotry.

GNORANCE, though not in the same category as fire and water, is a great destroyer of books. At the Reformation so strong was the antagonism of the people generally to anything like the old idolatry of the Romish Church, that they destroyed by thousands books, secular as well as sacred, if they contained but illuminated letters. Unable to read, they saw no difference between romance and a psalter, between King Arthur and King David; and so the paper books with all their artistic ornaments went to the bakers to heat their ovens, and the

parchment manuscripts, however beautifully illuminated, to the binders and boot makers.

There is another kind of ignorance which has often worked destruction, as shown by the following anecdote, which is extracted from a letter written in 1862 by M. Philarête Chasles to Mr. B. Beedham, of Kimbolton:—

> "Ten years ago, when turning out an old closet in the Mazarin Library, of which I am librarian, I discovered at the bottom, under a lot of old rags and rubbish, a large volume. It had no cover nor title-page, and had been used to light the fires of the librarians. This shows how great was the negligence towards our literary treasure before the Revolution; for the pariah volume, which, 60 years before, had been placed in the Invalides, and which had certainly formed part of the original Mazarin collections, turned out to be a fine and genuine Caxton."

I saw this identical volume in the Mazarin Library in April, 1880. It is a noble copy of the First Edition of the "Golden Legend," 1483, but of course very imperfect.

Among the millions of events in this world which cross and re-cross one another, remarkable coincidences must often occur; and a case exactly similar to that at the Mazarin Library, happened about the same time in London, at the French Protestant Church, St. Martin's-le-Grand. Many years ago I discovered there, in a dirty pigeon hole close to the grate in the vestry, a fearfully mutilated copy of Caxton's edition of the Canterbury Tales, with woodcuts. Like the book at Paris, it had long been used, leaf by leaf, in utter ignorance of its value, to light the vestry fire. Originally worth at least £800, it was then worth half, and, of course, I energetically drew the attention of the minister in charge to it, as well as to another grand Folio by Rood and Hunte, 1480. Some years elapsed, and then the Ecclesiastical Commissioners took the foundation in hand, but when at last Trustees were appointed, and the valuable library was re-arranged and catalogued, this "Caxton," together with the fine copy of "Latterbury" from the first Oxford Press, had disappeared entirely. Whatever ignorance may have been displayed in the mutilation, quite another word should be applied to the disappearance.

The following anecdote is so *apropos*, that although it has lately appeared in No. 1 of *The Antiquary*, I cannot resist the temptation of re-printing it, as a warning to inheritors of old libraries. The account was copied by me years ago from a letter written in 1847, by the Rev. C. F. Newmarsh, Rector of Pelham, to the Rev. S. R. Maitland, Librarian to the Archbishop of Canterbury, and is as follows :—

"In June, 1844, a pedlar called at a cottage in Blyton and asked an old widow, named Naylor, whether she had any rags to sell. She answered, No! but offered him some old paper, and took from a shelf the 'Boke of St. Albans' and others, weighing 9 lbs., for which she received 9*d.* The pedlar carried them through Gainsborough tied up in string, past a chemist's shop, who, being used to buy old paper to wrap his drugs in, called the man in, and, struck by the appearance of the 'Boke,' gave him 3*s*. for the lot. Not being able to read the Colophon, he took it to an equally ignorant stationer, and offered it to him for a guinea, at which price he declined it, but proposed that it should be exposed in his window as a means of eliciting some information about it. It was accordingly placed there with this label, 'Very old curious work.' A collector of books went in and offered half-a-crown for it, which excited the suspicion of the vendor. Soon after Mr. Bird, Vicar of Gainsborough, went in and asked the price, wishing to possess a very early specimen of printing, but not knowing the value of the book. While he was examining it, Stark, a very intelligent bookseller, came in, to whom Mr. Bird at once ceded the right of pre-emption. Stark betrayed such visible anxiety that the vendor, Smith, declined setting a price. Soon after Sir C. Anderson, of Lea (author of Ancient Models), came in and took away the book to collate, but brought it back in the morning having, found it imperfect in the middle, and offered £5 for it. Sir Charles had no book of reference to guide him to its value. But in the meantime, Stark had employed a friend to obtain for him the refusal of it, and had undertaken to give for it a little more than any sum Sir Charles might offer. On finding that at least £5 could be got for it, Smith went to the chemist and gave him two guineas, and then sold it to Stark's agent for seven guineas. Stark took it to London, and sold it at once to the Rt. Hon. Thos. Grenville for seventy pounds or guineas.

"I have now shortly to state how it came that a book without covers of such extreme age was preserved. About fifty years since, the library of Thonock Hall, in the parish of Gainsborough, the seat of the Hickman family, underwent great repairs, the books being sorted over by a most ignorant person, whose selection seems to have been determined by the coat. All books without covers were thrown into a great heap, and condemned to all the purposes which Leland laments in the sack of the conventual libraries by the visitors. But they found favour in the eyes of a literate gardener, who begged leave to take what he liked home. He selected a large quantity of Sermons preached before the House of Commons, local pamphlets, tracts from 1680 to 1710, opera books, etc. He made a list of them, which I found afterwards in the cottage. In the list, No. 43 was 'Cotarmouris,' or the Boke of St. Albans. The old fellow was something of a herald, and drew in his books what he held to be his coat. After his death, all that could be stuffed into a large chest were put away in a garret; but a few favourites, and the 'Boke' among them remained on the kitchen shelves for years, till his son's widow grew so 'stalled' of dusting them that she determined to sell them. Had she been in poverty, I should have urged the buyer, Stark, the duty of giving her a small sum out of his great gains."

Such chances as this do not fall to a man's lot twice; but Edmond Werdet relates a story very similar indeed, and where also the "plums" fell into the lap of a London dealer.

In 1775, the Recollet Monks of Antwerp, wishing to make a reform, examined their library, and determined to get rid of about 1,500 volumes—some manuscript and some printed, but all of which they considered as old rubbish of no value.

At first they were thrown into the gardener's rooms; but, after some months, they decided in their wisdom to give the whole refuse to the gardener as a recognition of his long services.

This man, wiser in his generation than these simple fathers, took the lot to M. Vanderberg, an amateur and man of education. M. Vanderberg took a cursory view, and then offered to buy them by weight at sixpence per pound. The bargain was at once concluded, and M. Vanderberg had the books.

Shortly after, Mr. Stark, a well-known London bookseller, being in Antwerp, called on M. Vanderberg, and was shown the books. He at once offered 14,000 francs for them, which was accepted. Imagine the surprise and chagrin of the poor monks when they heard of it! They knew they had no remedy, and so dumbfounded were they by their own ignorance, that they humbly requested M. Vanderberg to relieve their minds by returning some portion of his large gains. He gave them 1,200 francs.

The great Shakespearian and other discoveries, which were found in a garret at Lamport Hall in 1867 by Mr. Edmonds, are too well-known and too recent to need description. In this case mere chance seems to have led to the preservation of works, the very existence of which set the ears of all lovers of Shakespeare a-tingling.

In the summer of 1877, a gentleman with whom I was well acquainted took lodgings in Preston Street, Brighton. The morning after his arrival, he found in the w.c. some leaves of an old black-letter book. He asked permission to retain them, and enquired if there were any more where they came from. Two or three other fragments were found, and the landlady stated that her father, who was fond of antiquities, had at one time a chest full of old black-letter books; that, upon his death, they were preserved till she was tired of seeing them, and then, supposing them of no value, she had used them for waste; that for two years and a-half they had served for various household purposes, but she had just come to the end of them. The fragments preserved, and now in my possession, are a goodly portion of one of the most rare books from the press of Wynkyn de Worde, Caxton's successor. The title is a curious woodcut with the words

"Gesta Romanorum" engraved in an odd-shaped black letter. It has also numerous rude wood-cuts throughout. It was from this very work that Shakespeare in all probability derived the story of the three caskets which in "The Merchant of Venice" forms so integral a portion of the plot. Only think of that cloaca being supplied daily with such dainty bibliographical treasures!

In the Lansdowne Collection at the British Museum is a volume containing three manuscript dramas of Queen Elizabeth's time, and on a fly-leaf is a list of fifty-eight plays, with this note at the foot, in the handwriting of the well-known antiquary, Warburton:

> "After I had been many years collecting these Manuscript Playes, through my own carelessness and the ignorance of my servant, they was unluckely burned or put under pye bottoms."

Some of these "Playes" are preserved in print, but others are quite unknown and perished for ever when used as "pye-bottoms."

Mr. W. B. Rye, late Keeper of the Printed Books at our great National Library thus writes :—

"On the subject of ignorance you should some day, when at the British Museum, look at Lydgate's translation of Boccaccio's 'Fall of Princes,' printed by Pynson in 1494. It is 'liber rarissimus.' This copy when perfect had been very fine and quite uncut. On one fine summer afternoon in 1874 it was brought to me by a tradesman living at Lamberhurst. Many of the leaves had been cut into squares, and the whole had been rescued from a tobacconist's shop, where the pieces were being used to wrap up tobacco and snuff. The owner wanted to buy a new silk gown for his wife, and was delighted with three guineas for this purpose. You will notice how cleverly the British Museum binder has joined the leaves, making it, although still imperfect, a fine book."

Referring to the carelessness exhibited by some custodians of Parish Registers, Mr. Noble, who has had great experience in such matters, writes :—

"A few months ago I wanted a search made of the time of Charles I in one of the most interesting registers in a large town (which shall be nameless) in England. I wrote to the custodian of it, and asked him kindly to do the search for me, and if he was unable to read the names to get some one who understood the writing of that date to decipher the entries for me. I did not have a reply for a fortnight, but one morning the postman brought me a very large unregistered book-packet, which I found to be the original Parish Registers! He, however, addressed a note with it stating that he thought it best to send me the document itself to look at, and begged me to be good enough to return the Register to him as soon as done with. He evidently wished to serve me—his ignorance of responsibility without doubt proving his kindly disposition, and on that account alone I forbear to name him; but I can assure you I was heartily glad to have a letter from him in due time announcing that the precious documents were once more locked up in the parish chest. Certainly, I think such as he to be 'Enemies of books.' Don't you?"

Bigotry has also many sins to answer for. The late M. Müller, of Amsterdam, a bookseller of European fame, wrote to me as follows a few weeks before his death:—

"Of course, we also, in Holland, have many Enemies of books, and if I were happy enough to have your spirit and style I would try and write a companion volume to yours. Now I think the best thing I can do is to give you somewhat of my experience. You say that the discovery of printing has made the destruction of anybody's books difficult. At this I am bound to say that the Inquisition did succeed most successfully, by burning heretical books, in destroying numerous volumes invaluable for their wholesome contents. Indeed, I beg to state to you the amazing fact that here in Holland exists an Ultramontane Society called 'Old Paper,' which is under the sanction of the six Catholic Bishops of the Netherlands, and is spread over the whole kingdom. The openly-avowed object of this Society is to buy up and to destroy as waste paper all the Protestant and Liberal Catholic newspapers, pamphlets and books, the price of which is offered to the Pope as 'Deniers de St. Pierre.' Of course, this Society is very little known among Protestants, and many have denied even its existence; but I have been fortunate enough to obtain a printed circular issued by one of the Bishops containing statistics of the astounding mass of paper thus collected. producing in one district alone the sum of £1,200 in three months. I need not tell you that this work is strongly promoted by the Catholic clergy. You can have no idea of the difficulty we now have in procuring certain books published but 30, 40, or 50 years ago of an ephemeral character. Historical and theological books are very rare; novels and poetry of that period are absolutely not to be found; medical and law books are more common. I am bound to say that in no country have more books been printed and more destroyed than in Holland. W. MÜLLER."

The policy of buying up all objectionable literature seems to me, I confess, very short-sighted, and in most cases would lead to a greatly increased reprint; it certainly would in these latitudes.

From the Church of Rome to the Church of England is no great leap, and Mr. Smith, the Brighton bookseller, gives evidence thus :—

> "It may be worth your while to note that the clergy of the last two centuries ought to be included in your list (of Biblioclasts). I have had painful experience of the fact in the following manner. Numbers of volumes in their libraries have had a few leaves removed, and in many others whole sections torn out. I suppose it served their purpose thus to use the wisdom of greater men and that they thus economised their own time by tearing out portions to suit their purpose. The hardship to the trade is this: their books are purchased in good faith as perfect, and when resold the buyer is quick to claim damage if found defective, while the seller has no redress."

Among the careless destroyers of books still at work should be classed Government officials. Cart-loads of interesting documents, bound and unbound, have been sold at various times as waste-paper,[1] when modern red-tape thought them but rubbish. Some of them have been rescued and resold at high prices, but some have been lost for ever.

In 1854 a very interesting series of blue books was commenced by the authorities of the Patent Office, of course paid for out of the national purse. Beginning with the year 1617 the particulars of every important patent were printed from the original specifications and fac-simile drawings made, where necessary, for the elucidation of the text. A very moderate price was charged for each, only indeed the prime cost of production. The general public, of course, cared little for such literature, but those interested in the origin and progress of any particular art, cared

[1] Nell Gwyn's private Housekeeping Book was among them, containing most curious particulars of what was necessary in the time of Charles I for a princely household. Fortunately it was among the rescued, and is now in a private library.

much, and many sets of Patents were purchased by those engaged in research. But the great bulk of the stock was, to some extent, inconvenient, and so when a removal to other offices, in 1879, became necessary, the question arose as to what could be done with them. These blue-books, which had cost the nation many thousands of pounds, were positively sold to the paper mills as waste-paper, and nearly 100 tons weight were carted away at about £3 per ton. It is difficult to believe, although positively true, that so great an act of vandalism could have been perpetrated, even in a Government office. It is true that no demand existed for some of them, but it is equally true that in numerous cases, especially in the early specifications of the steam engine and printing machine, the want of them has caused great disappointment. To add a climax to the story, many of the "pulped" specifications have had to be reprinted more than once since their destruction.

CHAPTER VI.

The Bookworm.

HERE is a sort of busy worm
That will the fairest books deform,
By gnawing holes throughout them;
Alike, through every leaf they go,
Yet of its merits naught they know,
Nor care they aught about them.

Their tasteless tooth will tear and taint
The Poet, Patriot, Sage or Saint,
Not sparing wit nor learning.
Now, if you'd know the reason why,
The best of reasons I'll supply;
'Tis bread to the poor vermin.

Of pepper, snuff, or 'bacca smoke,
And Russia-calf they make a joke.
Yet, why should sons of science
These puny rankling reptiles dread?
'Tis but to let their books be read,
And bid the worms defiance."

J. Doraston.

A most destructive Enemy of books has been the bookworm. I say "has been," because, fortunately, his ravages in all civilised countries have been greatly restricted during the last fifty years. This is due partly to the increased reverence for antiquity which has been universally developed—more still to the feeling of cupidity, which has caused all owners to take care of volumes which year by year have become more valuable—and, to some considerable extent, to the falling off in the production of edible books.

The monks, who were the chief makers as well as the custodians of books, through the long ages we call "dark," because so little is known of them, had no fear of the bookworm before their eyes, for, ravenous as he is and was, he loves not parchment, and at that time paper was not. Whether at a still earlier period he attacked the papyrus, the paper of the Egyptians, I know not—probably he did, as it was a purely vegetable substance; and if so, it is quite possible that the worm of to-day, in such evil repute with us, is the lineal descendant of ravenous ancestors who plagued the sacred Priests of On in the time of Joseph's Pharoah, by destroying their title deeds and their books of Science.

Rare things and precious, as manuscripts were before the invention of typography, are well preserved, but when the printing press was invented and paper books were multiplied in the earth; when libraries increased and readers were many, then familiarity bred contempt; books were packed in out-of-the-way places and neglected, and the oft-quoted, though seldom seen, bookworm became an acknowledged tenant of the library, and the mortal enemy of the bibliophile.

Anathemas have been hurled against this pest in nearly every European language, old and new, and classical scholars of bye-gone centuries have thrown their spondees and dactyls at him. Pierre Petit, in 1683, devoted a long Latin poem to his dis-praise, and Parnell's charming Ode is well known. Hear the poet lament :—

> "Pene tu mihi passerem Catulli,
> Pene tu mihi Lesbiam abstulisti."

and then—

> "Quid dicam innumeros bene eruditos
> Quorum tu monumenta tu labores
> Isti pessimo ventre devorasti?"

while Petit, who was evidently moved by strong personal feelings against the "invisum pecus," as he calls him, addresses his little enemy as "Bestia audax" and "Pestis chartarum."

But, as a portrait commonly precedes a biography, the curious reader may wish to be told what this "Bestia audax," who so greatly ruffles the tempers of our eclectics, is like. Here, at starting, is a serious chameleon-like difficulty, for the bookworm offers to us, if we are guided by their words, as many varieties of size and shape as there are beholders.

Sylvester, in his "Laws of Verse," with more words than wit, described him as "a microscopic creature wriggling on the learned page, which, when discovered, stiffens out into the resemblance of a streak of dirt."

The earliest notice is in "Micrographia," by R. Hooke, folio, London, 1665. This work, which was printed at the expense of the Royal Society of London, is an account of innumerable things examined by the author under the microscope, and is most interesting for the frequent accuracy of the author's observations, and most amusing for his equally frequent blunders.

In his account of the bookworm, his remarks, which are rather long and very minute, are absurdly blundering. He calls it "a small white Silver-shining Worm or Moth, which I found much conversant among books and papers, and is supposed to be that which corrodes and eats holes thro' the leaves and covers. Its head appears bigg and blunt, and its body tapers from it towards the tail, smaller and smaller, being shap'd almost like a carret. . . . It has two long horns before, which are streight, and tapering towards the top, curiously ring'd or knobb'd and brisled much like the marsh weed called Horses tail. . . . The hinder part is terminated with three tails, in every particular resembling the two longer horns that grow out of the head. The legs are scal'd and hair'd. This animal probably feeds upon the paper and covers of books, and perforates in them several small round holes, finding perhaps a convenient nourishment in those husks of hemp and flax, which have passed through so many scourings, washings, dressings, and dryings as the parts of old paper necessarily have suffer'd. And, indeed, when I consider what a heap of sawdust or chips

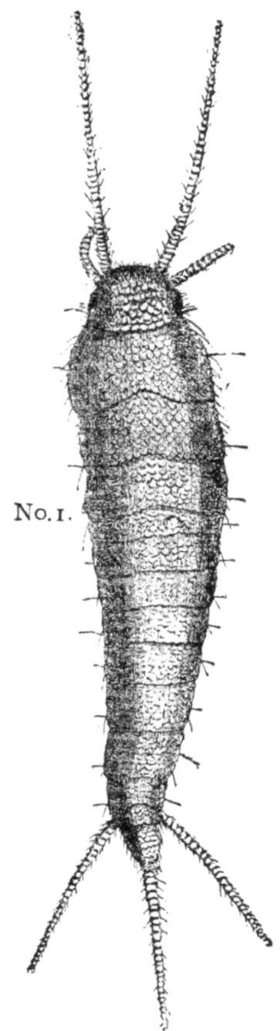

No. 1.—The image of the Bookworm as it is graven in "Micrographia," by R. Hooke, Fellow of the Royal Society.

Fo. London, 1665.

No. 2.—Anobium, natural size.

No. 3.—Anobium, magnified.

this little creature (which is one of the teeth of Time) conveys into its intrals, I cannot chuse but remember and admire the excellent contrivance of Nature in placing in animals such a fire, as is continually nourished and supply'd by the materials convey'd into the stomach and fomented by the bellows of the lungs." The picture or "image," which accompanies this description, is wonderful to behold. Certainly R. Hooke, Fellow of the Royal Society, drew somewhat upon his imagination here, having apparently evolved both engraving and description from his inner consciousness.[1]

Entomologists even do not appear to have paid much attention to the natural history of the "Worm." Kirby, speaking of it, says,

[1] Not so!. Several correspondents have drawn my attention to the fact that Hooke is evidently describing the "Lepisma," which, if not positively injurious, is often found in the warm places of old houses, especially if a little damp. He mistook this for the Bookworm.

"the larvæ of Crambus pinguinalis spins a robe which it covers with its own excrement, and does no little injury." Again, "I have often observed the caterpillar of a little moth that takes its station in damp old books, and there commits great ravages, and many a black-letter rarity, which in these days of bibliomania would have been valued at its weight in gold, has been snatched by these devastators," etc., etc.

As already quoted, Doraston's description is very vague. To him he is in one verse "a sort of busy worm," and in another "a puny rankling reptile." Hannett, in his work on book-binding, gives "Aglossa pinguinalis" as the real name, and Mrs. Gatty, in her Parables, christens it "Hypothenemus eruditus."

The Rev. F. T. Havergal, who many years ago had much trouble with bookworms in the Cathedral Library of Hereford, says they are a kind of death-watch, with a "hard outer skin, and are dark brown," another sort "having white bodies with brown spots on their heads." Mr. Holme, in "Notes and Queries" for 1870, states that the "Anobium paniceum" has done considerable injury to the Arabic manuscripts brought from Cairo, by Burckhardt, and now in the University Library, Cambridge. Other writers say "Acarus eruditus" or "Anobium pertinax" are the correct scientific names.

Personally, I have come across but few specimens; nevertheless, from what I have been told by librarians, and judging from analogy, I imagine the following to be about the truth:—

There are several kinds of caterpillar and grub, which eat into books, those with legs are the larvæ of moths; those without legs, or rather with rudimentary legs, are grubs and turn to beetles.

It is not known whether any species of caterpillar or grub can live generation after generation upon books alone, but several sorts of wood-borers, and others which live upon vegetable refuse, will attack paper, especially if attracted in the first place by the real wooden boards in which it was the custom of the old book-binders to clothe their volumes. In this belief, some country librarians object to opening the library windows lest the enemy should fly in from the neighbouring woods, and rear a brood of worms. Anyone, indeed, who has seen a hole in a filbert, or a piece of wood riddled by dry rot, will recognize a similarity of appearance in the channels made by these insect enemies.

Among the paper-eating species are:—

1. The "Anobium." Of this beetle there are varieties, viz.: "A. pertinax," "A. eruditus," and "A. paniceum." In the lava state they are grubs, just like those found in nuts; in this stage they are too much alike to be distinguished from one another. They feed on old dry wood, and often infest book-cases and shelves. They eat the wooden

boards of old books, and so pass into the paper where they make long holes quite round, except when they work in a slanting direction, when the holes appear to be oblong. They will thus pierce through several volumes in succession, Peignot, the well-known bibliographer, having found 27 volumes so pierced in a straight line by one worm, a miracle of gluttony, the story of which, for myself, I receive "*cum grano salis.*" After a certain time the larva changes into a pupa, and then emerges as a small brown beetle.

2. "Oecophora."—This larva is similar in size to that of Anobium, but can be distinguished at once by having legs. It is a caterpillar, with six legs upon its thorax and eight sucker-like protuberances on its body, like a silk-worm. It changes into a chrysalis, and then assumes its perfect shape as a small brown moth. The species that attacks books is the Œcophora pseudospretella. It loves damp and warmth, and eats any fibrous

material. This caterpillar is quite unlike any garden species, and, excepting the legs, is very similar in appearance and size to the Anobium. It is about half-inch long, with a horny head and strong jaws. To printers' ink or writing ink he appears to have no great dislike, though I imagine that the former often disagrees with his health, unless he is very robust, as in books where the print is pierced a majority of the worm-holes I have seen are too short in extent to have provided food enough for the development of the grub. But, although the ink may be unwholesome, many grubs survive, and, eating day and night in silence and darkness, work out their destiny leaving, according to the strength of their constitutions, a longer or shorter tunnel in the volume.

In December, 1879, Mr. Birdsall a well-known book-binder of Northampton, kindly sent me by post a fat little worm, which had been found by one of his workmen in an old book while being bound. He bore his journey extremely well, being very lively when turned out. I placed him in a box in warmth and quiet, with some small fragments of paper from a Boethius, printed by Caxton, and a leaf of a seventeeth century book. He ate a small piece of the leaf, but either from too much fresh air, from unaccustomed liberty, or from change of food, he gradually weakened, and died in about three weeks. I was sorry to lose him, as I wished to verify his name in his perfect state. Mr. Waterhouse, of the Entomological department of the British Museum, very kindly examined him before death, and was of opinion he was Œcophora pseudospretella.

In July, 1885, Dr. Garnett, of the British Museum, gave me two worms which had been found in an old Hebrew Commentary just received from Athens. They had doubtless had a good shaking on the journey, and one was moribund when I took charge, and joined his defunct kindred in a few days. The other seemed hearty and lived with me for nearly eighteen months. I treated him as well as I knew how; placed him in a small box with the choice of three sorts of old paper to eat, and very seldom disturbed him. He evidently resented his confinement, ate very little, moved very little, and changed in appearance very little, even when dead. This Greek worm, filled with Hebrew lore, differed in many respects from any other I have seen. He was longer, thinner, and more delicate looking than any of his English congeners. He was transparent, like thin ivory, and had a dark line through his body, which I took to be the intestinal canal. He resigned his life with extreme procrastination, and died "deeply lamented" by his keeper, who had long looked forward to his final development.

The difficulty of breeding these worms is probably due to their formation. When in a state of nature they can by expansion and contraction of the body working upon the sides of their holes, push their horny jaws against the opposing mass of paper. But when freed from the restraint, which indeed to them is life, they *cannot* eat although surrounded with food, for they have no legs to keep them steady, and their natural leverage is wanting.

Considering the numerous old books contained in the British Museum, the Library there is wonderfully free from the worm. Mr. Rye, lately the Keeper of the Printed Books there, writes me "Two or three were discovered in my time, but they were weakly creatures. One, I remember, was conveyed into the Natural History Department, and was taken into custody by Mr. Adam White who pronounced it to be Anobium pertinax. I never heard of it after."

The reader, who has not had an opportunity of examining old libraries, can have no idea of the dreadful havoc which these pests are capable of making.

I have now before me a fine folio volume, printed on very good unbleached paper, as thick as stout cartridge, in the year 1477, by Peter Schoeffer, of Mentz. Unfortunately, after a period of neglect in which it suffered severely from the "worm," it was about fifty years ago considered worth a new cover, and so again suffered severely, this time at the hands of the binder. Thus the original state of the boards is unknown, but the damage done to the leaves can be accurately described.

The "worms" have attacked each end. On the first leaf are 212 distinct holes, varying in size from a common pin hole to that which a stout knitting-needle would make, say, $\frac{1}{16}$ to $\frac{1}{23}$ inch. These holes run mostly in lines more or less at right angles with the covers, a very few being channels along the paper affecting three or four sheets only.

The varied energy of these little pests is thus represented :—

On folio	1 are	212 holes.		On folio	61	are	4	holes.
,,	11 ,,	57 ,,		,,	71	,,	2	,,
,,	21 ,,	48 ,,		,,	81	,,	2	,,
,,	31 ,,	31 ,,		,,	87	,,	1	,,
,,	41 ,,	18 ,,		,,	90		0	,,
,,	51 ,,	6 ,,						

These 90 leaves being stout, are about the thickness of 1 inch. The volume has 250 leaves, and turning to the end, we find on the last leaf 81 holes, made by a breed of worms not so ravenous. Thus,

From end.	From end.
On folio 1 are 81 holes.	On folio 66 is 1 hole.
,, 11 ,, 40 ,,	,, 69 ,, 0 ,,

It is curious to notice how the holes, rapidly at first, and then slowly and more slowly, disappear. You trace the same hole leaf after leaf, until suddenly the size becomes in one leaf reduced to half its normal diameter, and a close examination will show a small abrasion of the paper in the next leaf exactly where the hole would have come if continued. In the book quoted it is just as if there had been a race. In the first ten leaves the weak worms are left behind; in the second ten there are still forty-eight eaters; these are reduced to thirty-one in the third ten, and to only eighteen in the fourth ten. On folio 51 only six worms hold on, and before folio 61 two of them have given in. Before reaching folio 71 it is a neck and neck race between two sturdy gourmands, each making a fine large hole, one of them being oval in shape. At folio 71 they are still neck and neck, and at folio 81 the same. At folio 87 the oval worm gives in, the round one eating three more leaves and part way through the fourth. The leaves of the book are then untouched until we reach the sixty-ninth from the end, upon which is one worm hole. After this they go on multiplying to the end of the book.

I have quoted this instance because I have it handy, but many worms eat much longer holes than any in this volume; some I have seen running quite through a couple of thick volumes, covers and all. In the "Schoeffer" book the holes are probably the work of Anobium pertinax, because the centre is spared and both ends attacked. Originally, real wooden boards were the covers of the volume, and here, doubtless, the attack was commenced, which was carried through each board into the paper of the book.

I remember well my first visit to the Bodleian Library, in the year 1858, Dr. Bandinel being then the librarian. He was very kind, and afforded me every facility for examining the fine collection of "Caxtons," which was the object of my journey. In looking over a parcel of black-letter fragments, which had been in a drawer for a long time, I came across a small grub, which, without a thought, I threw on the floor and trod under foot.

Soon after I found another, a fat, glossy fellow, so long ——, which I carefully preserved in a little paper box, intending to observe his habits and development. Seeing Dr. Bandinel near, I asked him to look at my curiosity. Hardly, however, had I turned the wriggling little victim out upon the leather-covered table, when down came the doctor's great thumb-nail upon him, and an inch-long smear proved the tomb of all my hopes, while the great bibliographer, wiping his thumb on his coat sleeve, passed on with the remark, "Oh, yes! they have black heads sometimes." That was something to know—another fact for the entomologist; for my little gentleman had a hard, shiny, white head, and I never heard of a black-headed bookworm before or since. Perhaps the great abundance of black-letter books in the Bodleian may account for the variety. At any rate he was an Anobium.

I have been unmercifully "chaffed" for the absurd idea that a *paper*-eating worm could be kept a prisoner in a *paper* box. Oh, these critics! Your bookworm is a shy, lazy beast, and takes a day or two to recover his appetite after being "evicted." Moreover, he knew his own dignity better than to eat the "loaded" glazed shoddy note paper in which he was incarcerated.

In the case of Caxton's "Lyf of oure ladye," already referred to, not only are there numerous small holes, but some very large channels at the bottom of the pages. This is a most unusual occurrence, and is probably the work of the larva of "Dermestes vulpinus," a garden beetle, which is very voracious, and eats any kind of dry ligneous rubbish.

The scarcity of edible books of the present century has been mentioned. One result of the extensive adulteration of modern paper is that the worm will not touch it. His instinct forbids him to eat the china clay, the bleaches, the plaster of Paris, the sulphate of barytes, the scores of adulterants now used to mix with the fibre, and, so far, the wise pages of the old literature are, in the race against Time with the modern rubbish, heavily handicapped. Thanks to the general interest taken in old books now-a-days, the worm has hard times of it, and but slight chance of that quiet neglect which is necessary to his existence. So much greater is the reason why some patient entomologist should, while there is the chance, take upon himself to study the habits of the creature, as Sir John Lubbock has those of the ant.

I have now before me some leaves of a book, which, being waste, were used by our economical first printer, Caxton, to make boards, by pasting them together. Whether the old paste was an attraction, or whatever the reason may have been, the worm, when he got in there, did not, as usual, eat straight through everything into the middle of the book, but worked his way longitudinally, eating great furrows along the leaves without passing out of the binding; and so furrowed are these few leaves by long channels that it is difficult to raise one of them without its falling to pieces.

This is bad enough, but we may be very thankful that in these temperate climes we have no such enemies as are found in very hot countries, where a whole library, books, bookshelves, table, chairs, and all, may be destroyed in one night by a countless army of ants.

Our cousins in the United States, so fortunate in many things, seem very fortunate in this—their books are not attacked by the "worm"—at any rate, American writers say so. True it is that all their black-letter comes from Europe, and, having cost many dollars, is well looked after; but there they have thousands of seventeenth and eighteenth century books, in Roman type, printed in the States on genuine and wholesome paper, and the worm is not particular, at least in this country, about the type he eats through, if the paper is good.

Probably, therefore, the custodians of their old libraries could tell a different tale, which makes it all the more amusing to find in the excellent "Encyclopædia of Printing,"[1] edited and printed by Ringwalt, at Philadelphia, not only that the bookworm is a stranger there, for personally he is unknown to most of us, but that his slightest ravages are looked upon as both curious and rare. After quoting Dibdin, with the addition of a few flights of imagination of his own, Ringwalt states that this "paper-eating moth is supposed to have been introduced into England in hogsleather binding from Holland." He then ends with what, to anyone who has seen the ravages of the worm in hundreds of books, must be charming in its native simplicity. "There is now," he states, evidently quoting it as a great

[1] "American Encyclopædia of Printing": by J. Luther Ringwalt. 8vo. Philadelphia, 1871.

curiosity, "there is now, in a private library in Philadelphia, a book perforated by this insect." Oh! lucky Philadelphians! who can boast of possessing the oldest library in the States, but must ask leave of a private collector if they wish to see the one worm-hole in the whole city!

CHAPTER VII.

Other Vermin.

ESIDES the worm I do not think there is any insect enemy of books worth description. The domestic black-beetle, or cockroach, is far too modern an introduction to our country to have done much harm, though he will sometimes nibble the binding of books, especially if they rest upon the floor.

Not so fortunate, however, are our American cousins, for in the "Library Journal" for September, 1879, Mr. Weston Flint gives an account of a dreadful little pest which commits great havoc upon the cloth bindings of the New York libraries. It is a small black-beetle or cockroach, called by scientists "Blatta germanica" and by others the "Croton Bug." Unlike our household pest, whose home is the kitchen, and whose bashfulness loves secrecy and the dark hours, this misgrown flat species, of which it would take two to make a medium-sized English specimen, has gained in impudence what it has lost in size, fearing neither light nor noise, neither man nor beast. In the old English Bible of 1551, we read in Psalm xci, 5, "Thou shalt not nede to be afraied for eny Bugges by night." This verse falls unheeded on the ear of the Western librarian who fears his "bugs" both night and day, for they crawl over everything in broad sunlight, infesting and infecting each corner and cranny of the bookshelves they choose as their home. There is a remedy in the powder known as insecticide, which, however, is very disagreeable upon books and shelves. It is, nevertheless, very fatal to these pests, and affords some consolation in the fact that so soon as a "bug" shows any signs of illness, he is devoured at once by his voracious brethren with the same relish as if he were made of fresh paste.

There is, too, a small silvery insect (Lepisma) which I have often seen in the backs of neglected books, but his ravages are not of much importance.

Nor can we reckon the Codfish as very dangerous to literature, unless, indeed, he be of the Roman obedience, like that wonderful Ichthiobibliophage (pardon me, Professor Owen) who, in the year 1626, swallowed three Puritanical treatises of John Frith, the Protestant martyr. No wonder, after such a meal, he was soon caught, and became famous in the annals of literature. The following is the title of a little book issued upon the occasion: "Vox Piscis, or the Book-Fish containing Three Treatises, which were found in the belly of a Cod-Fish in Cambridge Market on Midsummer Eve, A°. 1626." Lowndes says (see under "Tracey,") "great was the consternation at Cambridge upon the publication of this work."

Rats and mice, however, are occasionally very destructive, as the following anecdote will show: Two centuries ago, the library of the Dean and Chapter of Westminster was kept in the Chapter House, and repairs having become necessary in that building, a scaffolding was erected inside, the books being left on their shelves. One of the holes made in the wall for a scaffold-pole was selected by a pair of rats for their family residence. Here they formed a nest for their young ones by descending to the library shelves and biting away the leaves of various books. Snug and comfortable was the little household, until, one day, the builder's men having finished, the poles were removed, and —alas! for the rats—the hole was closed up with bricks and cement. Buried alive, the father and mother, with five or six of their offspring, met with a speedy death, and not until a few years ago, when a restoration of the Chapter House was effected, was the rat grave opened again for a scaffold pole, and all their skeletons and their nest discovered. Their bones and paper fragments of the nest may now be seen in a glass case in the Chapter House, some of the fragments being attributed to books from the press of Caxton. This is not the case, although there are pieces of very early black-letter books not now to be found in the Abbey library, including little bits of the famous Queen Elizabeth's Prayer book, with woodcuts, 1568.

A friend sends me the following incident: "A few years since, some rats made nests in the trees surrounding my house; from thence they jumped on to some flat roofing, and so made their way down a chimney into a room where I kept books. A number of these,

Vermin.

with parchment backs, they entirely destroyed, as well as some half-dozen books whole bound in parchment."

Another friend informs me that in the Natural History Museum of the Devon and Exeter Institution is a specimen of "another little pest, which has a great affection for bindings in calf and roan. Its scientific name is Niptus Hololencus." He adds, "Are you aware that there was a terrible creature allied to these, rejoicing in the name of Tomicus Typographus, which committed sad ravages in Germany in the seventeenth century, and in the old liturgies of that country is formally mentioned under its vulgar name, 'The Turk'?" (See Kirby and Spence, Seventh Edition, 1858, p. 123.) This is curious, and I did not know it, although I know well that Typographus Tomicus, or the "cutting printer," is a sad enemy of (good) books. Upon this part of our subject, however, I am debarred entering.

The following is from W. J. Westbrook, Mus. Doc., Cantab., and represents ravages with which I am personally unacquainted:

"Dear Blades,—I send you an example of the 'enemy'-mosity of an ordinary house-fly. It hid behind the paper, emitted some caustic fluid, and then departed this life. I have often caught them in such 'holes.' 30/12/83."

The damage is an oblong hole, surrounded by a white fluffy glaze (fungoid ?), difficult to represent in a wood-cut. The size here given is exact.

Chapter VIII.

Bookbinders.

N the first chapter I mentioned bookbinders among the Enemies of Books, and I tremble to think what a stinging retort might be made if some irate bibliopegist were to turn the scales on the printer, and place *him* in the same category. On the sins of printers, and the unnatural neglect which has often shortened the lives of their typographical progeny, it is not for me to dilate. There is an old proverb, "'Tis an ill bird that befouls its own nest"; a curious chapter thereupon, with many modern examples, might nevertheless be written. This I will leave, and will now only place on record some of the cruelties

perpetrated upon books by the ignorance or carelessness of binders.

Like men, books have a soul and body. With the soul, or literary portion, we have nothing to do at present; the body, which is the outer frame or covering, and without which the inner would be unusable, is the special work of the binder. He, so to speak, begets it; he determines its form and adornment, he doctors it in disease and decay, and, not unseldom, dissects it after death. Here, too, as through all Nature, we find the good and bad running side by side. What a treat it is to handle a well-bound volume; the leaves lie open fully and freely, as if tempting you to read on, and you handle them without fear of their parting from the back. To look at the "tooling," too, is a pleasure, for careful thought, combined with artistic skill, is everywhere apparent. You open the cover and find the same loving attention inside that has been given to the outside, all the workmanship being true and thorough. Indeed, so conservative is a good binding, that many a worthless book has had an honoured old age, simply out of respect to its outward aspect; and many a real treasure has come to a degraded end and premature death through the unsightliness of its outward case and the irreparable damage done to it in binding.

The weapon with which the binder deals the most deadly blows to books is the "plough," the effect of which is to cut away the margins, placing the print in a false position relatively to the back and head, and often denuding the work of portions of the very text. This reduction in size not seldom brings down a handsome folio to the size of quarto, and a quarto to an octavo.

With the old hand plough a binder required more care and caution to produce an even edge throughout than with the new cutting machine. If a careless workman found that he had not ploughed the margin quite square with the text, he would put it in his press and take off "another shaving," and sometimes even a third.

Dante, in his "Inferno," deals out to the lost souls various tortures suited with dramatic fitness to the past crimes of the victims, and had I to execute judgment on the criminal binders of certain precious volumes I have seen, where the untouched maiden sheets entrusted to their care have, by barbarous treatment, lost dignity, beauty and value, I would collect the paper shavings so ruthlessly shorn off, and roast the perpetrator of the outrage over their slow combustion. In olden times, before men had learned to value the relics of our printers, there was some excuse for the sins of a binder who erred from ignorance which was general; but in these times, when the historical and antiquarian value of old books is freely acknowledged, no quarter should be granted to a careless culprit.

It may be supposed that, from the spread of information, all real danger from ignorance is past. Not so, good reader; that is a consummation as yet "devoutly to be wished." Let me relate to you a true bibliographical anecdote: In 1877, a certain lord, who had succeeded to a fine collection of old books, promised to send some of the most valuable (among which were several Caxtons) to the Exhibition at South Kensington. Thinking their outward appearance too shabby, and not knowing the danger of his conduct, he decided to have them rebound in the neighbouring county town. The volumes were soon returned in a resplendent state, and, it is said, quite to the satisfaction of his lordship, whose pleasure, however, was sadly damped when a friend pointed out to him that, although the discoloured edges had all been ploughed off, and the time-stained blanks, with their fifteenth century autographs, had been replaced by nice clean fly-leaves, yet, looking at the result in its lowest aspect only—that of market value—the books had been damaged to at least the amount of £500; and, moreover, that caustic remarks would most certainly follow upon their public exhibition. Those poor injured volumes were never sent.

Some years ago one of the most rare books printed by Machlinia—a thin folio—was discovered bound in sheep by a country bookbinder, and cut down to suit the size of some quarto tracts. But do not let us suppose that country binders are the only culprits. It is not very long since the discovery of a unique Caxton in one of our largest London libraries. It was in boards, as originally issued by the fifteenth-century binder, and a great fuss (very properly) was made over the treasure trove. Of course, cries the reader, it was kept in its original covers, with all the interesting associations of its early state untouched? No such thing!

Instead of making a suitable case, in which it could be preserved just as it was, it was placed in the hands of a well-known London binder, with the order, "Whole bind in velvet." He did his best, and the volume now glows luxuriously in its gilt edges and its inappropriate covering, and, alas! with half-an-inch of its uncut margin taken off all round. How do I know that? because the clever binder, seeing some MS. remarks on one of the margins, turned the leaf down to avoid cutting them off, and that stern witness will always testify, to the observant reader, the original size of the book. This same binder, on another occasion, placed a unique fifteenth century Indulgence in warm water, to separate it from the cover upon which it was pasted, the result being that, when dry, it was so distorted as to be useless. That man soon after passed to another world, where, we may hope, his works have not followed him, and that his merits as a good citizen and an honest man counterbalanced his de-merits as a binder.

Other similar instances will occur to the memory of many a reader, and doubtless the same sin will be committed from time to time by certain binders, who seem to have an ingrained antipathy to rough edges and large margins, which of course are, in their view, made by Nature as food for the shaving tub.

De Rome, a celebrated bookbinder of the eighteenth century, who was nicknamed by Dibdin "The Great Cropper," was, although in private life an estimable man, much addicted to the vice of reducing the margins of all books sent to him to bind. So far did he go, that he even spared not a fine copy of Froissart's Chronicles, on vellum, in which was the autograph of the well-known book-lover, De Thou, but cropped it most cruelly.

Owners, too, have occasionally diseased minds with regard to margins. A friend writes: "Your amusing anecdotes have brought to my memory several biblioclasts whom I have known. One roughly cut the margins off his books with a knife, hacking away very much like a hedger and ditcher. Large paper volumes were his especial delight, as they gave more paper. The slips thus obtained were used for index-making! Another, with the bump of order unnaturally developed, had his folios and quartos all reduced, in binding, to one size, so that they might look even on his bookshelves."

This latter was, doubtless, cousin to him who deliberately cut down all his books close to the text, because he had been several times annoyed by readers who made marginal notes.

The indignities, too, suffered by some books in their lettering! Fancy an early black-letter fifteenth-century quarto on Knighthood, labelled "Tracts"; or a translation of Virgil, "Sermons"! The "Histories of Troy," printed by Caxton, still exists with "Eracles" on the back, as its title, because that name occurs several times in the early chapters, and the binder was too proud to seek advice. The words "Miscellaneous," or "Old Pieces," were sometimes used when binders were at a loss for lettering, and many other instances might be mentioned.

The rapid spread of printing throughout Europe in the latter part of the fifteenth century caused a great fall in the value of plain un-illuminated MSS., and the immediate consequence of this was the destruction of numerous volumes written upon parchment, which were used by the binders to strengthen the backs of their newly-printed rivals. These slips of vellum or parchment are quite common in old books. Sometimes whole sheets are used as fly-leaves, and often reveal the existence of most valuable works, unknown before—proving, at the same time, the small value formerly attached to them.

Many a bibliographer, while examining old books, has to his great puzzlement come across short slips of parchment, nearly always from some old manuscript, sticking out like "guards" from the midst of the leaves. These suggest, at first, imperfections or damage done to the volume; but if examined closely it will be found that they are always in the middle of a paper section, and the real reason of their existence is just the same as when two leaves of parchment occur here and there in a paper volume, viz.: strength—strength to resist the lug which the strong thread makes against the middle of each section. These slips represent old books destroyed, and like the slips already noticed, should always be carefully examined.

When valuable books have been evil-entreated, when they have become soiled by dirty hands, or spoiled by water stains, or injured by grease spots, nothing is more astonishing to the uninitiated than the transformation they undergo in the hands of a skilful restorer. The covers are first carefully dissected, the eye of the operator keeping a careful outlook for any fragments of old MSS. or early printed books, which may have been used by the original binder. No force should be applied to separate parts which adhere together; a little warm water and care is sure to overcome that difficulty. When all the sections are loose, the separate sheets are placed singly in a bath of cold water, and allowed to remain there until all the dirt has soaked out. If not sufficiently purified, a little hydrochloric or oxalic acid, or caustic potash may be put in the water, according as the stains are from grease or from ink. Here is where an unpractised binder will probably injure a book for life. If the chemicals are too strong, or the sheets remain too long in the bath, or are not thoroughly cleansed from the bleach before they are re-sized, the certain seeds of decay are planted in the paper, and although for a time the leaves may look bright to the eye, and even crackle under the hand like the soundest paper, yet in the course of a few years the enemy will appear, the fibre will decay, and the existence of the books will terminate in a state of white tinder.

Everything which diminishes the interest of a book is inimical to its preservation, and in fact is its enemy. Therefore, a few words upon the destruction of old bindings.

I remember purchasing many years ago at a suburban book stall, a perfect copy of Moxon's Mechanic Exercises, now a scarce work. The volumes were uncut, and had the original marble covers. They looked so attractive in their old fashioned dress, that I at once determined to preserve it. My binder soon made for them a neat wooden box in the shape of a book, with morocco back properly lettered, where I trust the originals will be preserved from dust and injury for many a long year.

Old covers, whether boards or paper, should always be retained if in any state approaching decency. A case, which can be embellished to any extent looks every whit as well upon the shelf! and gives even greater protection than binding. It has also this great advantage: it does not deprive your descendants of the opportunity of seeing for themselves exactly in what dress the book buyers of four centuries ago received their volumes.

CHAPTER IX.

Collectors.

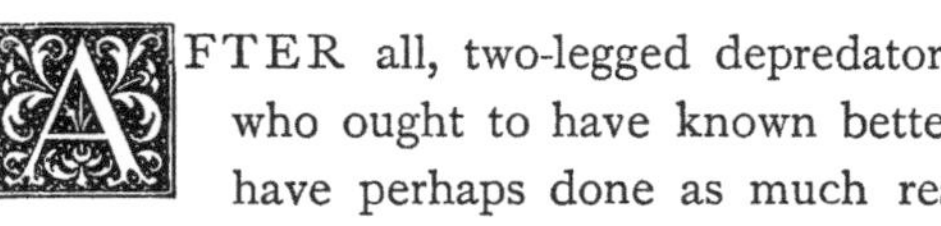

AFTER all, two-legged depredators, who ought to have known better, have perhaps done as much real damage in libraries as any other enemy. I do not refer to thieves, who, if they injure the owners, do no harm to the books themselves by merely transferring them from one set of bookshelves to another. Nor do I refer to certain readers who frequent our public libraries, and, to save themselves the trouble of copying, will cut out whole articles from magazines or encyclopædias. Such depredations are not frequent, and only occur with books easily replaced, and do not therefore call for more than a passing mention; but it is a serious matter when Nature produces such a wicked old biblioclast as John Bagford, one of the founders of the Society of Antiquaries, who, in the beginning of the last century, went about the country, from library to library, tearing away title pages from rare books of all sizes. These he sorted out into nationalities and towns, and so, with a lot of hand-bills, manuscript notes, and miscellaneous collections of all kinds, formed over a hundred folio volumes, now preserved in the British Museum. That they are of service as materials in compiling a general history of printing cannot be denied, but the destruction of many rare books was the result, and more than counter-balanced any benefit bibliographers will ever receive from them. When here and there throughout those volumes you meet with titles of books now either unknown entirely, or of the greatest rarity; when you find the Colophon from the end, or the "insignum typographi" from the first leaf of a rare "fifteener," pasted down with dozens of others, varying in value, you cannot bless the memory of the antiquarian shoemaker, John Bagford. His portrait, a half-length, painted by Howard, was engraved by Vertue, and re-engraved for the Bibliographical Decameron.

A bad example often finds imitators, and every season there crop up for public sale one or two such collections, formed by bibliomaniacs, who, although calling themselves bibliophiles, ought really to be ranked among the worst enemies of books.

The following is copied from a trade catalogue, dated April, 1880, and affords a fair idea of the extent to which these heartless destroyers will go :—

"MISSAL ILLUMINATIONS.

FIFTY DIFFERENT CAPITAL LETTERS *on* VELLUM; *all in rich Gold and Colours. Many*

3 *inches square: the floral decorations are of great beauty, ranging from the XIIth to XVth century. Mounted on stout card-board.* IN NICE PRESERVATION, £6 6*s*.

These beautiful letters have been cut from precious MSS., and as specimens of early art are extremely valuable, many of them being worth 15*s*. each."

Mr. Proëme is a man well known to the London dealers in old books. He is wealthy, and cares not what he spends to carry out his bibliographical craze, which is the collection of title pages. These he ruthlessly extracts, frequently leaving the decapitated carcase of the books, for which he cares not, behind him. Unlike the destroyer Bagford, he has no useful object in view, but simply follows a senseless kind of classification. For instance: One set of volumes contains nothing but copper-plate engraved titles, and woe betide the grand old Dutch folios of the seventeenth century if they cross his path. Another is a volume of coarse or quaint titles, which certainly answer the end of showing how idiotic and conceited some authors have been. Here you find Dr. Sib's "Bowels opened in Divers Sermons," 1650, cheek by jowl with the discourse attributed falsely to Huntington, the Calvinist, "Die and be damned," with many others too coarse to be quoted. The odd titles adopted for his poems by Taylor, the water-poet, enliven several pages, and make one's mouth water for the books themselves. A third volume includes only such titles as have the printer's device. If you shut your eyes to the injury done by such collectors, you may, to a certain extent, enjoy the collection, for there is great beauty in some titles; but such a pursuit is neither useful nor meritorious. By and by the end comes, and then dispersion follows collection, and the volumes, which probably cost £200 each in their formation, will be knocked down to a dealer for £10, finally gravitating into the South Kensington Library, or some public museum, as a bibliographical curiosity. The following has just been sold (July, 1880) by Messrs. Sotheby, Wilkinson and Hodge, in the Dunn-Gardinier collection, lot 1592 :—

"TITLEPAGES AND FRONTISPIECES.

A Collection of upwards of 800 ENGRAVED TITLES AND FRONTISPIECES, ENGLISH AND FOREIGN *(some very fine and curious) taken from old books and neatly mounted on cartridge paper in 3 vol. half morocco gilt. imp. folio.*"

The only collection of title-pages which has afforded me unalloyed pleasure is a handsome folio, published by the directors of the Plantin Museum, Antwerp, in 1877, just after the purchase of that wonderful typographical storehouse. It is called "Titels en Portretten gesneden naar P. P. Rubens voor de Plantijnsche Drukkerij," and it contains thirty-five grand title pages, reprinted from the original seventeenth century plates, designed by Rubens himself between the years 1612 and 1640, for various publications which issued from the celebrated Plantin Printing Office. In the same Museum are preserved in Rubens' own handwriting his charge for each design, duly receipted at foot.

I have now before me a fine copy of "Cōclusiones siue decisiones antique dñor' de Rota," printed by Gutenberg's partner, Schoeffer, in the year 1477. It is perfect, except in a most vital part, the Colophon, which has been cut out by some barbaric "Collector," and which should read thus: "Pridie nonis Januarii Mccccl xxvij, in Civitate Moguntina, impressorie Petrus Schoyffer de Gernsheym," followed by his well-known mark, two shields.

A similar mania arose at the beginning of this century for collections of illuminated initials, which were taken from MSS., and arranged on the pages of a blank book in alphabetical order. Some of our cathedral libraries suffered severely from depredations of this kind. At Lincoln, in the early part of this century, the boys put on their robes in the library, a room close to the choir. Here were numerous old MSS., and eight or ten rare Caxtons. The choir boys used often to amuse themselves, while waiting for the signal to "fall in," by cutting out with their pen-knives the illuminated initials and vignettes, which they would take into the choir with them and pass round from one to another. The Dean and Chapter of those days were not much better, for they let Dr. Dibdin have all their Caxtons for a "consideration." He made a little catalogue of them, which he called "A Lincolne Nosegaye." Eventually they were absorbed into the collection at Althorp.

The late Mr. Caspari was a "destroyer" of books. His rare collection of early woodcuts, exhibited in 1877 at the Caxton Celebration, had been frequently augmented by the purchase of illustrated books, the plates of which were taken out, and mounted on Bristol boards, to enrich his collection. He once showed me the remains of a fine copy of "Theurdanck," which he had served so, and I have now before me several of the leaves which he then gave me, and which, for beauty of engraving and cleverness of typography, surpasses any typographical work known to me. It was printed for the Emperor Maximilian, by Hans Schonsperger, of Nuremberg, and, to make it unique, all the punches were cut on purpose, and as many as seven or eight varieties of each letter, which, together with the clever way in which the ornamental flourishes are carried above and below the line, has led even experienced printers to deny its being typography. It is, nevertheless, entirely from cast types. A copy in good condition costs about £50.

Many years since I purchased, at Messrs. Sotheby's, a large lot of MS. leaves on vellum, some being whole sections of a book, but mostly single leaves. Many were so mutilated by the excision of initials as to be worthless, but those with poor initials, or with none, were quite good, and when sorted out I found I had got large portions of nearly twenty different MSS., mostly Horæ, showing twelve varieties of fifteenth century handwriting in Latin, French, Dutch, and German. I had each sort bound separately, and they now form an interesting collection.

Portrait collectors have destroyed many books by abstracting the frontispiece to add to their treasures, and when once a book is made imperfect, its march to destruction is rapid. This is why books like Atkyns' "Origin and Growth of Printing," 4to, 1664, have become impossible to get. When issued, Atkyns' pamphlet had a fine frontispiece, by Logan, containing portraits of King Charles II, attended by Archbishop Sheldon, the Duke of Albermarle, and the Earl of Clarendon.

As portraits of these celebrities (excepting, of course, the King) are extremely rare, collectors have bought up this 4to tract of Atkyns', whenever it has been offered, and torn away the frontispiece to adorn their collection. This is why, if you take up any sale catalogue of old books, you are certain to find here and there, appended to the description, "Wanting the title," "Wanting two plates," or "Wanting the last page."

It is quite common to find in old MSS., especially fifteenth century, both vellum and paper, the blank margins of leaves cut away. This will be from the side edge or from the foot, and the recurrence of this mutilation puzzled me for many years. It arose from the scarcity of paper in former times, so that when a message had to be sent which required more exactitude than could be entrusted to the stupid memory of a household messenger, the Master or Chaplain went to the library, and, not having paper to use, took down an old book, and cut from its broad margins one or more slips to serve his present need.

I feel quite inclined to reckon among "enemies" those bibliomaniacs and over-careful possessors, who, being unable to carry their treasures into the next world, do all they can to hinder their usefulness in this. What a difficulty there is to obtain admission to the curious library of old Samuel Pepys, the well-known diarist. There it is at Magdalene College, Cambridge, in the identical book-cases provided for the books by Pepys himself; but no one can gain admission except in company of two Fellows of the College, and if a single book be lost, the whole library goes away to a neighbouring college. However willing and anxious to oblige, it is evident that no one can use the library at the expense of the time, if not temper, of two Fellows. Some similar restrictions are in force at the Teylerian Museum, Haarlem, where a lifelong imprisonment is inflicted upon its many treasures.

Some centuries ago a valuable collection of books was left to the Guildford Endowed Grammar School. The schoolmaster was to be held personally responsible for the safety of every volume, which, if lost, he was bound to replace. I am told that one master, to minimize his risk as much as possible, took the following barbarous course:—As soon as he was in possession, he raised the boards of the schoolroom floor, and, having carefully packed all the books between the joists, had the boards nailed down again. Little recked he how many rats and mice made their nests there; he was bound to account some day for every single volume, and he saw no way so safe as rigid imprisonment.

The late Sir Thomas Phillipps, of Middle Hill, was a remarkable instance of a biblio-taph. He bought bibliographical treasures simply to bury them. His mansion was crammed with books; he purchased whole libraries, and never even saw what he had bought. Among some of his purchases was the first book printed in the English language, "The Recuyell of the Histories of Troye," translated and printed by William Caxton, for the Duchess of Burgundy, sister to our Edward IV. It is true, though almost incredible, that Sir Thomas could never find this volume, although it is doubtless still in the collection, and no wonder, when cases of books bought twenty years before his death were never opened, and the only knowledge of their contents which he possessed was the Sale Catalogue or the bookseller's invoice.

CHAPTER X.

SERVANTS AND CHILDREN.

EADER! are you married? Have you offspring, boys especially I mean, say between six and twelve years of age? Have you also a literary workshop, supplied with choice tools, some for use, some for ornament, where you pass pleasant hours? and is—ah! there's the rub!—is there a special hand-maid, whose special duty it is to keep your den daily dusted and in order? Plead you guilty to these indictments? then am I sure of a sympathetic co-sufferer.

Dust! it is all a delusion. It is not the dust that makes women anxious to invade the inmost recesses of your Sanctum—it is an ingrained curiosity. And this feminine weakness, which dates from Eve, is a common motive in the stories of our oldest literature and Folk-lore. What made Fatima so anxious to know the contents of the room forbidden her by Bluebeard? It was positively nothing to her, and its contents caused not the slightest annoyance to anybody. That story has a bad moral, and it would, in many ways, have been more satisfactory had the heroine been left to take her place in the blood-stained chamber, side by side with her peccant predecessors. Why need the women-folk (God forgive me!) bother themselves about the inside of a man's library, and whether it wants dusting or not? My boys' playroom, in which is a carpenter's bench, a lathe, and no end of litter, is never tidied—perhaps it can't be, or perhaps their youthful vigour won't stand it—but *my* workroom must needs be dusted daily, with the delusive promise that each book and paper shall be replaced exactly where it was. The damage done by such continued treatment is incalculable. At certain times these observances are kept more religiously than others; but especially should the book-lover, married or single, beware of the Ides of March. So soon as February is dead and gone, a feeling of unrest seizes the housewife's mind. This increases day by day, and becomes dominant towards the middle of the month, about which period sundry hints are thrown out as to whether you are likely to be absent for a day or two. Beware! the fever called "Spring Clean" is on, and unless you stand firm, you will rue it. Go away, if the Fates so will, but take the key of your own domain with you.

Do not misunderstand. Not for a moment would I advocate dust and dirt; they are enemies, and should be routed; but let the necessary routing be done under your own eye. Explain where caution must be used, and in what cases tenderness is a virtue; and if one Eve in the family can be indoctrinated with book-reverence you are a happy man; her price is above that of rubies; she will prolong your life. Books *must* now and then be taken clean out of their shelves, but they should be tended lovingly and with judgment. If the dusting can be done just outside the room so much the better. The books removed, the shelf should be lifted quite out of its bearings, cleansed and wiped, and then each volume should be taken separately, and gently rubbed on back and sides with a soft cloth. In returning the volumes to their places, notice should be taken of the binding, and especially when the books are in whole calf or morocco care should be taken not to let them rub together. The best bound books are soonest injured, and quickly deteriorate in bad company. Certain volumes, indeed, have evil tempers, and will scratch the faces of all their neighbours who are too familiar with them. Such are books with metal clasps and rivets on their edges; and such, again, are those abominable old rascals, chiefly born in the fifteenth century, who are proud of being dressed in *real* boards with brass corners, and pass their lives with fearful knobs and metal bosses, mostly five in number, firmly fixed on one of their sides. If the tendencies of such ruffians are not curbed, they will do as much mischief to their gentle neighbours as when a "collie" worries the sheep. These evil results may always be minimized by placing a piece of millboard between the culprit and his victim. I have seen lovely bindings sadly marked by such uncanny neighbours.

When your books are being "dusted," don't impute too much common sense to your assistants; take their ignorance for granted, and tell them at once never to lift any book by one of its covers; that treatment is sure to strain the back, and ten to one the weight will be at the same time miscalculated, and the volume will fall. Your female "help," too, dearly loves a good tall pile to work at, and, as a rule, her notions of the centre of gravity are not accurate, leading often to a general downfall, and the damage of many a corner. Again, if not supervised and instructed, she is very apt to rub the dust into, instead of off, the edges. Each volume should be held tightly, so as to prevent the leaves from gaping, and then wiped from the back to the fore-edge. A soft brush will be found useful if there is much dust. The whole exterior should also be rubbed with a soft cloth, and then the covers should be opened and the hinges of the binding examined; for mildew *will* assert itself both inside and outside certain books, and that most pertinaciously. It has unaccountable likes and dislikes. Some bindings seem positively to invite damp, and mildew will attack these when no other books on the same shelf show any signs of it. When discovered, carefully wipe it away, and then let the book remain a few days standing open, in the driest and airiest spot you can select. Great care should be taken not to let grit, such as blows in at the open window from many a dusty road, be upon your duster, or you will probably find fine scratches, like an outline map of Europe, all over your smooth calf, by which your heart and eye, as well as your book, will be wounded.

"Helps" are very apt to fill the shelves too tightly, so that to extract a book you have to use force, often to the injury of the top-bands. Beware of this mistake. It frequently occurs through not noticing that one small book is purposely placed at each end of the shelf, beneath the movable shelf-supports, thus not only saving space, but preventing the injury which a book shelf-high would be sure to receive from uneven pressure.

After all, the best guide in these, as in many other matters, is "common sense," a quality which in olden times must have been much more "common" than in these days, else the phrase would never have become rooted in our common tongue.

Children, with all their innocence, are often guilty of book-murder. I must confess to having once taken down "Humphrey's History of Writing," which contains many brightly-coloured plates, to amuse a sick daughter. The object was certainly gained, but the consequences of so bad a precedent were disastrous. That copy (which, I am glad to say, was easily re-placed), notwithstanding great care on my part, became soiled and torn, and at last was given up to Nursery martyrdom. Can I regret it? surely not, for, although bibliographically sinful, who can weigh the amount of real pleasure received, and actual pain ignored, by the patient in the contemplation of those beautifully-blended colours?

A neighbour of mine some few years ago suffered severely from a propensity, apparently irresistible, in one of his daughters to tear his library books. She was six years old, and would go quietly to a shelf and take down a book or two, and having torn a dozen leaves or so down the middle, would replace the volumes, fragments and all, in their places, the damage being undiscovered until the books were wanted for use. Reprimand, expostulation and even punishment were of no avail; but a single "whipping" effected a cure.

Boys, however, are by far more destructive than girls, and have, naturally, no reverence for age, whether in man or books. Who does not fear a schoolboy with his first pocket-knife? As Wordsworth did not say:—

"You may trace him oft
By scars which his activity has left
Upon our shelves and volumes. * * *
He who with pocket-knife will cut the edge
Of luckless panel or of prominent book,
Detaching with a stroke a label here, a back-band there."

Excursion III, 83.

Pleased, too, are they, if, with mouths full of candy, and sticky fingers, they can pull in and out the books on your bottom shelves, little knowing the damage and pain they will cause. One would fain cry out, calling on the Shade of Horace to pardon the false quantity—

> "Magna movet stomacho fastidia, si puer unctis
> Tractavit volumen manibus." *Sat. IV.*

What boys *can* do may be gathered from the following true story, sent me by a correspondent who was the immediate sufferer:—

One summer day he met in town an acquaintance who for many years had been abroad; and finding his appetite for old books as keen as ever, invited him home to have a mental feed upon "fifteeners" and other bibliographical dainties, preliminary to the coarser pleasures enjoyed at the dinner-table. The "home" was an old mansion in the outskirts of London, whose very

Children.

architecture was suggestive of black-letter and sheep-skin. The weather, alas! was rainy, and, as they approached the house, loud peals of laughter reached their ears. The children were keeping a birthday with a few young friends. The damp forbad all outdoor play, and, having been left too much to their own devices, they had invaded the library. It was just after the Battle of Balaclava, and the heroism of the combatants on that hard-fought field was in everybody's mouth. So the mischievous young imps divided themselves into two opposing camps—Britons and Russians. The Russian division was just inside the door, behind ramparts formed of old folios and quartos taken from the bottom shelves and piled to the height of about four feet. It was a wall of old fathers, fifteenth century chronicles, county histories, Chaucer, Lydgate, and such like. Some few yards off were the Britishers, provided with heaps of small books as missiles, with which they kept up a skirmishing cannonade against the foe. Imagine the tableau! Two elderly gentlemen enter hurriedly, paterfamilias receiving, quite unintentionally, the first edition of "Paradise Lost" in the pit of his stomach, his friend narrowly escaping a closer personal acquaintance with a quarto Hamlet than he had ever had before. Finale: great outburst of wrath, and rapid retreat of the combatants, many wounded (volumes) being left on the field.

POSTSCRIPTUM.

LTHOUGH, strictly speaking, the following anecdote does not illustrate any form of real injury to books, it is so racy, and in these days of extravagant biddings so tantalizing, that I must step just outside the strict line of pertinence in order to place it on record. It was sent to me, as a personal experience, by my friend, Mr. George Clulow, a well-known bibliophile, and "Xylographer" to "Ye Sette of ye Odde Vǫlumes." The date is 1881. He writes:—

"*Apropos* of the Gainsborough 'find,' of which you tell in 'The Enemies of Books,' I should like to narrate an experience of my own, of some twenty years ago:

"Late one evening, at my father's house, I saw a catalogue of a sale of furniture, farm implements and books, which was announced to take place on the following morning at a country rectory in Derbyshire, some four miles from the nearest railway station.

"It was summer time—the country at its best—and with the attraction of an old book, I decided on a day's holiday, and eight o'clock the next morning found me in the train for C——, and after a variation in my programme, caused by my having walked three miles west before I discovered that my destination was three miles east of the railway station, I arrived at the rectory at noon, and found assembled some thirty or forty of the neighbouring farmers, their wives, men-servants and maid-servants, all seemingly bent on a day's idling, rather than business. The sale was announced for noon, but it was an hour later before the auctioneer put in an appearance, and the first operation in which he took part, and in which he invited my assistance, was to make a hearty meal of bread and cheese and beer in the rectory kitchen. This over, the business of the day began by a sundry collection of pots, pans, and kettles being brought to the competition of the public, followed by some lots of bedding, etc. The catalogue gave books as the first part of the sale, and, as three o'clock was reached, my patience was gone, and I protested to the auctioneer against his not selling in accordance with his catalogue. To this he replied that there was not time enough, and that he would sell the books to-morrow! This was too much for me, and I suggested that he had broken faith with the buyers, and had brought me to C—— on a false pretence. This, however, did not seem to disturb his good humour, or to make him unhappy, and his answer was to call 'Bill,' who was acting as porter, and to tell him to give the gentleman the key of the 'booāk room,' and to bring down any of the books he might pick out, and he 'would sell 'em.' I followed 'Bill,' and soon found myself in a charming nook of a library, full of books, mostly old divinity, but with a large number of the best miscellaneous literature of the sixteenth century, English and foreign. A very short look over the shelves produced some thirty Black Letter books, three or four illuminated missals, and some book rarities of a more recent date. 'Bill' took them downstairs, and I wondered what would happen! I was not long in doubt, for book by book, and in lots of two and three, my selection was knocked down in rapid succession, at prices varying from 1*s.* 6*d.* to 3*s.* 6*d.*, this latter sum seeming to be the utmost limit to the speculative turn of my competitors. The *bonne bouche* of the lot was, however, kept back by the auctioneer, because, as he said, it was 'a pretty book,' and I began to respect his critical judgment, for 'a pretty book' it was, being a large paper copy of Dibdin's Bibliographical Decameron, three volumes, in the original binding. Suffice it to say that, including this charming book, my purchases did not amount to £13, and I had pretty well a cart-load of books for my money—more than I wanted much! Having brought them home, I 'weeded them out,' and the 'weeding' realised four times what I gave for the whole, leaving me with some real book treasures.

"Some weeks afterwards I heard that the remainder of the books were literally treated as waste lumber, and carted off to the neighbouring town, and were to be had, any one of them, for sixpence, from a cobbler who had allowed his shop to be used as a store house for them. The news of their being there reached the ears of an old bookseller in one of the large towns, and he, I think, cleared out the lot. So curious an instance of the most total ignorance on the part of the sellers, and I may add on the part of the possible buyers also, I think is worth noting."

How would the reader in this Year of Grace, 1887, like such an experience as that?

Conclusion.

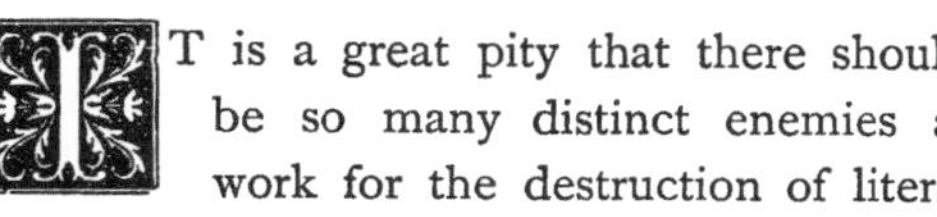

T is a great pity that there should be so many distinct enemies at work for the destruction of literature, and that they should so often be allowed to work out their sad end. Looked at rightly, the possession of any old book is a sacred trust, which a conscientious owner or guardian would as soon think of ignoring as a parent would of neglecting his child. An old book, whatever its subject or internal merits, is truly a portion of the national history; we may imitate it and print it in fac-simile, but we can never exactly reproduce it; and as an historical document it should be carefully preserved.

I do not envy any man that absence of sentiment which makes some people careless of the memorials of their ancestors, and whose blood can be warmed up only by talking of horses or the price of hops. To them solitude means *ennui*, and anybody's company is preferable to their own. What an immense amount of calm enjoyment and mental renovation do such men miss. Even a millionaire will ease his toils, lengthen his life, and add a hundred per cent. to his daily pleasures if he becomes a bibliophile; while to the man of business with a taste for books, who through the day has struggled in the battle of life with all its irritating rebuffs and anxieties, what a blessed season of pleasurable repose opens upon him as he enters his sanctum, where every article wafts to him a welcome, and every book is a personal friend!

INDEX.

For EU product safety concerns, contact us at Calle de José Abascal, 56–1°, 28003 Madrid, Spain or eugpsr@cambridge.org.

www.ingramcontent.com/pod-product-compliance
Ingram Content Group UK Ltd.
Pitfield, Milton Keynes, MK11 3LW, UK
UKHW012343130625
459647UK00009B/493

* 9 7 8 1 1 0 8 0 7 6 4 1 8 *